Referral Mastery

37 Exact Ways to Ask for a Referral and Get It Every Time!

By Joe Stumpf

Referral Master: 37 Exact Ways to Ask for a Referral and Get It Every Time!
By Joe Stumpf
 First edition 2014

By Referral Only, Inc.
2035 Corte Del Nogal, Suite 200
Carlsbad, CA 92011
www.byreferralonly.com

Table of Contents

Here's what's inside...

- *Exact Way to Ask 11* – How to Use a Six-Word Pattern That Quickly Interrupts to Plant a Referral Seed
- *Exact Way to Ask 12* – Be the Strong Person They're Looking for to Overcome Procrastination
- *Exact Way to Ask 13* – Master Both Parts of Every Transaction
- *Exact Way to Ask 14* – How to Use Confusion to Your Advantage
- *Exact Way to Ask 15* – Get a Referral from Those Who Are Easiest to Get It From!
- *Exact Way to Ask 16* – How to Get Your Top Inactive Referral Prospects to Introduce You
- *Exact Way to Ask 17* – How to Know with 100% Certainty If the Person You Are Talking to Will Ever Introduce You!
- *Exact Way to Ask 18* – the Dialogue You MUST Use Before You EVER Talk About Your Compensation!
- *Exact Way to Ask 19* – Master the Art of Showing Clients the Selfish Benefit They Get for Referring You!
- *Exact Way to Ask 20* – How to Make Someone Comfortable with a Future Pacing Question
- *Exact Way to Ask 21* – Use This Simple Dialogue At a Party to Let Everyone Know Who You Are
- *Exact Way to Ask 22* – Use Three Degrees of Separation to Generate Infinite Numbers of Referrals!
- *Exact Way to Ask 23* – Don't Ask for NEW Referrals, Be Grateful for the Ones You Already Have
- *Exact Way to Ask 24* – Discover the Most Powerful Analogy That Will Make It Easier for Your Client to Refer You!

- *Exact Way to Ask 25* – The Easiest Way to Start a Casual Referral Conversation in Any Social Setting that Will Result in a Constant Stream of Referred Leads!
- *Exact Way to Ask 26* – Twenty-Four Words that Generated $4,500 in Commission in Less than 30 Seconds
- *Exact Way to Ask 27* – How to Make Sure People Don't Think You're Too Busy for Them
- *Exact Way to Ask 28* – Ask People for Their Advice and They'll Help You Get Business!
- *Exact Way to Ask 29* – "Who's the Next Person You Know that Is Most Likely to Sell Their House?"
- *Exact Way to Ask 30* – How to Turn Every Compliment into a Chance for a Referral
- *Exact Way to Ask 31* – How to Finally Deal with People Who Don't Refer!
- *Exact Way to Ask 32* – How to Handle "I Just Don't Know Anyone that I Can Refer to You."
- *Exact Way to Ask 33* – How to Make Them Feel Good About Introducing You Without Being Pushy
- *Exact Way to Ask 34* – How to Talk to Their Unconscious Concerns
- *Exact Way to Ask 35* – Everyone You Know Knows Someone Who Needs a Great Agent or Lender
- *Exact Way to Ask 36* – Help People Discover Places Where They Can Find People Who Need Your Help
- *Exact Way to Ask 37* – How to Become Highly Skilled During Moments of Awkward Silence

Introduction to Referral Mastery

How to Know If You Have "Referral Resistance" That's Dramatically Hurting Your Business

It's true. You probably have some level of resistance when it comes to asking for referrals in a consistent and predictable manner. And that could be dramatically hurting your business.

The first step in any improvement process is to honestly assess yourself and find out how much room you have for improvement. That's why I've created the "Referral Resistance" Assessment.

As you mindfully answer these 10 questions, there is a good chance you will open your awareness and learn how much better you can become.

"Referral Resistance" Assessment

1) Have you ever forgotten to ask for referrals?

   Yes or No

2) When meeting with a client do you spend too much time talking about current business...leaving you without enough time to ask for referrals?

   Yes or No

3) Do you feel awkward or uncomfortable when you ask for a referral and they don't know anyone?

Yes or No

4) Do you feel that asking for a referral is a sign of weakness and believe that if they know anyone they will refer you without you having to ask?

Yes or No

5) Do you ever feel that asking for a referral is unprofessional?

Yes or No

6) Have you ever felt like you were begging or groveling for business when you were asking for referrals?

Yes or No

7) Has a bad experience asking for a referral in the past made you decide not to do it anymore in the future?

Yes or No

8) Are you uncomfortable with the scripts or dialogues you use to ask for referrals or have you not had any training in asking for referrals?

Yes or No

9) Do you ever feel you don't deserve referrals?

Yes or No

10) Do you feel that most people have had a bad experience referring a friend to a typical salesperson so you don't bother asking?

Yes or No

If you answered yes to any of these questions, you may have "Referral Resistance!"

The good news is you can cure it with "Referral Mastery" now that you have the Referral Mastery program.

Imagine that eventually you will confidently answer "NO" to all ten of these questions and you will be well on your way to owning a "By Referral Only" business

The 5 Referral Mastery Mindsets

How to Use the 5 Referral Mindsets to Get Unlimited High Quality Prospects

Here's a serious mistake I see time and time again. Trying to simply memorize great scripts and dialogues rather than working on having the right MINDSET to gain referrals.

You can have all the words in the world, but if you don't have the right mindset, you'll only tap into a very small percentage of your referral opportunity.

That's why it's essential to make asking for referrals the DNA of your business.

But using the "Referral Mastery Mindset" to build your real estate or mortgage business is more than simply asking a few clients for referrals on a periodic basis.

So what is it?

It's an attitude and a way of thinking that needs to be ingrained into the very core of your entire business.

Let's start with the 5 Referral Mindsets. Embracing these mindsets is the first step in creating a systematic referral process that can help you get an unlimited supply of high quality prospects.

Mindset 1

Deepen Your Commitment to Referrals

What's the difference between interest and commitment?

Think about the hobbies that interested you. What comes to mind first?

Now, think of one thing in your life that you're really committed to. What's the first thing you think of?

Can you feel the difference between your two answers?

Most likely the things you are interested in are something you do when all the circumstances are perfect.

For example, I am interested in boogie boarding in the Pacific Ocean. When it comes to jumping in the ocean, whether or not I do it depends upon the circumstances.

I am much more interested when the weather is 80 degrees, the ocean temperature is 70 degrees and a friend is able to join me. Under these circumstances... let's hit the waves!

If the temperature is 68 degrees and the water is 54 degrees, then I'm not interested.

CrossFit comes to mind first when I think of something I am committed to.

My goal in 2014 is to qualify for the CrossFit World Wide Games. To qualify you must be in the top 20 in the world. I finished 21st in 2012 and 42nd in 2013.

I have organized my daily plan around training 3 hours a day, 6 days a week. I train with heavyweight for strength. I do interval training for stamina. I also do a CrossFit "Workout of the Day" 4 to 5 days a week.

In fact I'm so committed I actually live in a home across the street from a CrossFit box.

Can you feel my enthusiasm and excitement through my sharing this with you? What you're feeling is my commitment.

What Do Boogie-Boarding and CrossFit Have to Do with Getting More Referrals?

Here's the answer.

If you treat referrals like I treat my boogie boarding, then you'll only go after referrals when conditions are perfect. and that means you're not committed to making them a core part of your business.

See the difference?

On the other hand, if you COMMIT to making referrals the purpose of your business, then you won't WAIT for the right circumstances to show themselves.

What will you do instead?

Well, for one thing you become a student of the school of referrals.

You read and re-read "*Referral Mastery* ", you study each of the 5 Mindsets, 9 Amplifiers and 37 Ways to Ask, you take full advantage of all the referral coaching available to you, you watch the coaching videos and you listen incessantly to your "Referral Mastery Audios".

In other words you build your life around doing business By Referral Only.

That's commitment!

This mindset means you are committed to creating an experience so refreshing, so healthy and so joyful for your client that all they want to do is refer you to the people they care about because they feel your commitment to them.

Better still…

When you are committed to Referral Mastery you build the step-by-step systems that will AUTOMATICALLY generate referrals for your business. And you'll quickly become a master of Referral Dialogue

What's the True Purpose of Your Business?

I like to ask the agents and lenders that I teach: What is the single word that best sums up the ultimate focus for their business?

The words I hear most frequently are 'service' and 'profit'.

Then I like to suggest a word that better encompasses everything they want for a highly profitable and sustainable business. I'm sure you know what that word is…

Referral.

If you were to define the purpose of your business with just word…with the best word possible…that word would be REFERRAL.

Think about it.

If you have a plumbing problem, would you rather look in the yellow pages or contact a plumber that you are referred to?

So what about profitability?

Building a referral business costs you literally nothing in marketing, since the marketing is done by people who like, know and trust you.

And if you're worried about service, then realize that in order for people to refer you they must receive value that is remarkable. Which means they are willing to remark about what they received to others in a positive, powerful way.

Consider that the reason you're really in business is to create an experience that people are so outrageously happy with that all they want to do is refer you to the people they care about.

Here's another way to say it:

Your primary purpose in business is to BE on purpose because...

Your purpose is who you are.

And when your purpose is to show up in all your client relationships with your advice, knowledge, wisdom, love, compassion, systems, procedures, and all your actions leading to one very simple outcome – then your client respects and trust you so deeply that they refer you to the people they care about most.

Only when you commit to that conscious purpose do you create extraordinary referral results.

How do I know for certain?

I have been teaching referral marketing to real estate and mortgage professionals for a quarter of a century. Over three quarters of a million people have attended one or more of my workshops, listened to my tapes or read my blogs daily.

I can say with confidence that the biggest difference between being a highly referable real estate or mortgage consultant vs. taking referrals from time to time is the level of commitment you have towards building a referral business.

The question to ask yourself is: **Are you willing to make a conscious choice that Referral Mastery is the purpose of your business?**

I have a lifelong commitment to creating new ideas, new thoughts, new insights and new strategies on how to get more referrals.

That is my commitment.

Are you willing to join me?

Taking an occasional referral is easy. It requires little commitment and not much energy.

Here's what's harder and takes true commitment and energy...

Having a flow of 10 to 15, five-star referral prospects a month, every month, who seek your advice and counsel.

Are you willing to invest whatever it takes?

If you want to be a highly referable real estate or mortgage consultant, then there's only one answer...

YES.

Be careful of self-defeating questions like...

How much longer will this take before I start getting a steady stream of referrals?

Or...

How many more times do I have to ask before they actually refer someone to me?

If you want to become a high achieving By Referral Only Consultant, the amount of time and effort to obtain something worthwhile is secondary.

As you read and re-read *Referral Mastery,* keep asking yourself how you can step up your commitment to being referable and building referable relationships.

Then be willing to do whatever it takes!

Mindset 2

Develop a Referable Consciousness

So now that you're fully committed, how do you actually change your ability to make your business By Referral Only?

A change in your ability to get referrals depends on a change to your state of consciousness.

What is consciousness?

According to the Webster Dictionary, consciousness is awareness, sensitivity, and the ability to perceive the relationship between oneself and one's environment.

You use your conscious mind whenever you are thinking logically or carefully.

Before you can begin to ask for referrals you need to develop what I call "conscious referable behavior." Behaviors such as:

- Being conscious about telling the truth, no matter what!
- Being conscious about being on time!
- Consciously becoming more interested than trying to be interesting.
- Consciously increasing your acknowledgement of people through handwritten notes.
- Being conscious enough to quickly admit when you are wrong.
- Being conscious enough to say 'please' and 'thank you' more frequently.

- Consciously giving people permission to share how they feel about your service.

Can you see what makes these conscious referable behaviors? They're all things that will get you referrals by actively thinking and remembering to do these things.

For example when you are conscious enough to be on time, it indicates to clients how you will behave during the transaction and throughout the relationship.

Referral consciousness means always telling the truth even when it's more convenient for you not to! This strengthens your character and integrity.

Referral Consciousness means doing what you say you're going to do because you keep your commitments.

Are you starting to get this now?

Here's Why You Need Clear Relationship Boundaries to Have Referral Consciousness

Just like countries have borders, you have boundaries.

Imagine that boundaries are invisible lines you draw around yourself that shape your interactions with others. Just like countries have borders that help shape their values and culture.

Borders and boundaries are similar because they are necessary in order to structure and unify the way we run a business or country.

And if you don't communicate your boundaries clearly to your clients, you can't expect them to know what they are. The only place you can read minds is in a marriage, and sometimes that doesn't work very well either.

Being conscious of your boundaries means you can encourage collaborative, respectful behavior when a person or client enters into your life. It means you are able to communicate clearly—before a person enters into relationship with you—how you define a healthy, supportive relationship.

Imagine what will happen if you're NOT conscious of your boundaries.

Think about the interruptions and distractions that will cause you to lose focus and energy.

It's as simple as being aware of how important it is to teach people how to treat you.

When you are conscious of your boundaries, you are much more likely to gain the referrals of five-star prospects—those who are open, friendly, know what they want, will do it soon, and will work with you.

Why not remove all the problems that 'cost' you in terms of time, money, energy, and inner peace by consciously setting your boundaries?

Mindset 3

Build Character and Integrity

Do you think it's true that people of high character refer others like them to other people of high character?

It's an interesting question, is it not?

And if it's true, then here's the question you need to be asking:

How high is your character?

I know, it's not any easy question to answer. And you've probably never considered it before.

Take this quiz:

- Name the ten wealthiest people in the world.
- Name the last ten Heisman trophy winners.
- Name the last ten winners of the Miss America contest.
- How about the last ten Academy Award winners for best picture?
- The last decade's worth of World Series winners?

How'd you do?

I didn't do well either.

With the exception of you trivia hounds, none of us remembers much about the headliners of yesterday.

Surprising how quickly we forget, isn't it?

And what I've listed are not second-rate achievements.

The answers are the best people in their fields. But the applause dies. Awards tarnish. Achievements are forgotten. And accolades and certificates are buried with their owners.

Now, here's another quiz:

- Think of three people you enjoy spending time with.
- Name three people who have taught you something worthwhile.
- Name two friends who have helped you in a difficult time.
- List a few teachers who have aided your journey through school.
- Name a half-dozen heroes whose stories have inspired you.

Easier?

It was for me, too.

So what's the lesson?

The people who make a difference aren't the ones with the credentials, but the ones with character and integrity.

Your character and integrity defines how you stand up for your values, morals, and ethics. It demonstrates how your boundaries "translate" into actions. It's being who you appear to be because you're authentic and honoring your commitment to build the kind of business and life you choose for yourself and your family.

When your purpose and boundaries are clear, it's easier to make good decisions because your character and integrity guides (and simplifies) your choices like the point of True North on a compass.

Why is this so important to your ability to get referrals?

Because your business practices and the behavior that you display in the process of running your business will identify you as either being referable or not. Sooner or later your outward behavior indicates the kind of person you are on the inside.

The clearer you become about how and with whom you choose to work with, the more you'll attract the type of high-quality, compatible clients you seek.

And when your boundaries, purpose and integrity are in alignment and demonstrated during your day-to-day consulting, you're referable!

Mindset 4

Rise above Your Fears of Asking for Referrals

Where does fear come from?

To get past your fear of asking for a referral you need to understand the answer to this question. In my experience there are five places fear of referrals originate:

Fear occurs when you ask for a referral from a place of weakness, like when you're asking because you need a referral.

This means you're probably thinking: "Boy, I really need some referrals," and you're coming from a place of neediness.

Here's what you should be thinking instead:

"I'm asking because I AM referable. I really believe that what I offer people is extraordinary. I don't need the referral, I want it. And if they give it to me, great! If they don't, that's okay, too."

When you lean on people like you really need their referrals, you come from a place of weakness which causes your fear to rise, because now they can reject you.

Can you see the difference?

Fear occurs when you haven't provided enough value to a client and you ask that client for a referral.

When you know your consulting, negotiating and transactional oversight have not been strong with a particular client, and then you ask them for a referral, you are probably thinking something like this in the back of your mind...

"I didn't return your phone call six times and I messed up on including the washer and dryer, and now I'm asking for a referral?"

Can you see how this would create fear? It's because you are asking when you don't feel valuable.

Fear occurs when you haven't yet planted the seeds for that referral.

If you haven't planted the seeds for a referral in previous conversations with your client, it means this is the first time you're talking about it. And that can create fear.

It also increases the likelihood of a rejection. So you need to be really conscious to prepare your client for *the ask* in advance.

Fear occurs when you ask for a referral before you ask for comfort.

A really good habit to get into is this: Before you ever ask for an introduction from you client, ask them if they're comfortable first. Here's an example of what that looks like:

"Hey, next time you're talking to someone who wants to get a larger space, would you be comfortable introducing me to that person so I can help them?"

Ask for that first and I promise your fear will start to lessen. It's the opposite of the following approach which can induce fear:

"Hey, next time you're in a conversation with a person who wants to buy a home, would you introduce them to me?"

The reason this brings up more fear is because you're not asking the question you really want them answer, which is:

"Hey, are you guys comfortable introducing me to the people that you care about?"

Once you know your client is comfortable with a referral, then it is much easier for you to ask them for one.

Fear occurs when your unconscious programming is stacked with limiting beliefs.

Your beliefs create your reality. If you have limiting beliefs about your ability to successfully ask for a referral, then you are likely to create situations in which you are unable to receive them.

The only reason your beliefs have power over you is because you have decided they are true. But beliefs are only the same thoughts repeated over and over again in your head. Which means you can change them.

In order to make sure you don't have limiting beliefs, pay attention to your thoughts about asking for referrals. If they are negative, ask yourself why.

How to Easily Hypnotize Yourself to Never Be Fearful Again!

How do you know when it's fear talking?

It's when that little voice in your head says: *"I don't know if I should say that."*

Or: *"I don't know if I should call him."* Or maybe your inner voice is telling you: *"If I said that, he might not like me."*

That little voice starts to get louder and you start to hesitate or procrastinate. That's fear.

Your power to overcome fear comes from practicing focused affirmations.

One of the ways to bust through fear is to say:

I'm free of fear. I love reminding myself that I've managed to come through everything that has ever happened in my life. And right now it's really worth noticing that real estate markets come and go, and sometimes they're up and sometimes they're down. It's funny how some people choose to worry about things they have no control over, like the market. Experience shows that fears, worries and anxieties only come when a person imagines unpleasant things in the past or in the future. When I allow myself to get present, I realize that all is well right now. As Roosevelt said, there is nothing to fear except fear itself.

Just having a new thought can create a positive feeling and produce a new behavior. You can also say:

I am By Referral Only. That means I have to ask. Because I love myself, I constantly behave and think about how truly referable I am right now. I am on the cutting edge of referrability. My consulting, my negotiating and my organizational skills make it easy and joyful for people to love introducing me to the people that they love. I am By Referral Only.

Notice as you read that out loud, that you actually start to feel a little bit better!

The More You Affirm the Higher Version of Yourself the More Fear Starts to Shrink!

In Neuro-Linguistic Programming (NLP) there is a language pattern called the *swish pattern.* I use it frequently. I'll just close my eyes and get a picture of the very fearful experience that I'm imagining.

I'll get that picture in my mind, then I'll shrink it to make it small like it's going from playing on a 26-inch TV screen to a 12-inch TV...until it's just a small window playing in the bottom right hand corner of my screen. Then I bring up a screen right on top of that one, of the image that I want.

Then I practice shrinking and enlarging the two images —the fear image and the preferred image. I'll enlarge the fear window, while shrinking the preferred image down to a window on the left. Then back again, enlarging the preferred image and shrinking the fear again down to the right. Back and forth, good up, bad down, bad up, good down. I'm concentrating on being able to control the thought.

Once I get a sense that this fear is a thought I can expand or shrink, then I'm controlling it. It's not controlling me. As soon as I get that, I can take the next step of swishing it away. To do that, I can take the bad image, blow it up real big, and then just swish it, like I'm knocking it right off the screen. Then I can bring up the good image and let it remain as the main picture.

You could do that with practice pretty fast. You can just get the bad picture, get the good picture, blow it up, shrink it, blow it up, shrink it again. Decide you're in control now: blow up the bad, swish, bring up the good—OK, you're done!

Don't you want to control your mind as opposed to having your mind control you?

Fear is when the mind is taking control as opposed to you taking control of the mind. Affirmation gives you a sense of mind control.

Mindset 5

Referral Mastery Makes Others Feel Good!

Here's something you might not realize...

The number one reason people recommend people they care about is because it makes *them* feel good.

So what does this mean for you?

You need to know how to elicit good feelings in others.

One way to do that is to help them imagine how good they'll feel when they refer you. Your conversation with them will go like this:

"Imagine how good you'll feel when you introduce the people you care about to a person you really trust. Imagine how good you'll feel when your friends thank you for introducing them to a person like me who can help them. Imagine how good you'll feel when you know that your family, and friends are getting advice they can count on to make their dreams come true."

Did you notice what I did there?

I repeated the same phrase I wanted the client to remember. If you do that, you'll be able to imprint a pattern within your client. Here's an example I use when I'm talking to my friends:

"Imagine how good you're going to feel when you take the time to introduce people to the Referral Mastery Program and they call you up and say, 'Hey, thank you for encouraging me to get the Referral Mastery Program. It's really great.' Imagine how good you're going to feel."

I'm using the words "imagine" and "feel good" to build rapport. Rapport is something that happens in the unconscious mind. Helping people feel good builds rapport.

How to Turn Your Client's Negatives into Positives…Instantly!

When it comes to motivation about buying a home or giving a referral or doing anything else deeply important, it can be both a feeling clients want to have and a feeling they want to avoid. People can—at the same time—want to do something and want to avoid doing it.

Your buyers and sellers can get confused.

"We really want to buy a house, but we're not sure we're ready."

"I really feel like I'd like to own a home, but I can't afford it."

Here's the secret to turning these mixed feelings around in your favor. You flip the parts of the sentence before and after "but," because you never want people to end on a feeling you want them to avoid. That's because the last thing they say is what goes into their unconscious.

So when somebody says, *"I really feel like we should own a home, but I don't feel like we can afford it,"* you say to them: *"So what I hear you saying is you feel that you can't afford it, but you feel like you'd really like to own a home."*

Did you see the flip? Did you see how easy that was?

Always leave people with the feeling they want to move towards versus the feeling they're trying to avoid. You'll notice the opportunity to flip the "but" on its head in almost every conversation, and the people that you're communicating with will hardly even notice it. It will just go into their unconscious and they'll just feel better.

They'll go, "Yes, that's how we feel," and they'll feel better because when they talk about what they want versus what they're trying to avoid, they just naturally feel better. It's happening at the unconscious level.

For now, imagine yourself being an expert with these Magic Word dialogues. Just imagine that. Imagine feeling confident. Imagine yourself feeling good for no good reason at all.

The spiritual teacher Ram Dass said something really profound. He said he was working in villages and communities where there was a lot of child abuse going on, and they would go into these communities, and they would take the children out of these abusive families.

The children would scream for their parents because they only knew abuse. That's all they were familiar with, and because they were so familiar with that feeling — which means that they were not aware of any other feeling —they just screamed to get back to what they were familiar with.

What you're going to notice is that the feelings that become most familiar are the behaviors that have become ritualistic in your life. Even if it doesn't feel good, you do what you're familiar with.

In order to imagine "what it would be like to live in a home like that," your client has to move into the house through their imagination and feel it.

Now, what happens when I say to you...

"Imagine what it would feel like when you have mastery of these dialogues."

Something is happening in your mind right now when I say that to you. Just by suggesting those words, there's a certain level of joy that starts to appear within you. You begin to feel good.

How to Make Sure Clients ALWAYS Associate Good Feelings with YOU

Whenever you're working with people, your intention should always be to have them feel good when they're with you. If you're calling someone and giving them good or bad news on the phone, always leave them feeling better than before they picked up the phone.

Leave them with this experience...

"When I talk to Joe, I feel good."

You should always project clients into a future good feeling. Why?

Because the number one reason people refer those they care about to a service or a product is because referring makes *them* feel good.

I remember passionately referring my friend Dean to the whole line of Apple products. Dean was a PC guy for a long time and I converted to Apple long before he did.

I would say, *"Dean, come on, get with the act here. You are in the dark ages with the PC. Step into the Apple world."*

One day, he ventured out, and he got a Mac, and he called me up and said, *"What was I waiting for? It's like I took it out of the box, plugged it in, all the drives were there and I was up and going within 15 minutes."*

Today he's a Mac fan. He's encouraging everybody to be an Apple fanboy. I've been watching Dean share that with people and it makes me feel good that I influenced him.

Your job is to keep helping people imagine what it's going to feel like when their sister, cousin, or brother calls in a few weeks and says, *"Thank you so much for introducing me to Joe. He helped us buy the home of our dreams. We got a big bedroom for our son and we're in the school district we wanted, and we're so grateful for that."*

When somebody says, *"Here's my brother's information, give him a call, he wants your help,"* what are they really saying?

They're saying, make me feel good. Call my brother. Make me a hero to my brother so the next time I talk to my brother I feel good.

Your responsibility is to help people feel good about introducing people they care about to you.

Remember to use this phrase: "Imagine how good you'll feel..."

The 9 Referral Mastery Amplifiers

Amplifier 1

Increase Your Chances of a Referral By 50% with a Well-Orchestrated Introduction

Here's the scoop...

A well-orchestrated introduction may increase the chances of you getting a referral by more than 50%.

What do I mean by a "well-orchestrated" introduction?

When you give somebody your business card and say, *"Hey, can you have your friend give me call,"* the chances of that actually happening diminish significantly with every second. Here's why:

Everyone knows another real estate agent or lender. The person they want to introduce you to more than likely knows somebody else, so it's incumbent on you to create an introduction.

What does a great intro look like?

You: *"I'm wondering would it be okay for us to talk about the best ways to introduce your friend to me?"*

"Yes, that'd be fine."

"Well, if you were me and you wanted to get into a conversation with your friend, what do you think would be the best way to do that?"

So the first question you're going to ask is: *"Would you do it?"*

And then you want to know: *"How would we do it?"*

When people are asked to predict whether they're going to engage in something in the future, saying "yes" to it means they are more likely to keep the commitment to do it.

This was proven in recent elections when people were asked if they would vote in the upcoming election. People who said yes were 80% more likely to vote than those who weren't asked the same question…they were keeping their commitment.

You'll find that good pollsters or good campaigns are always saying, *"Vote. Get out and vote. Will you vote?"* Then as soon as people agree to vote they ask, *"Would you vote for me?"* They don't start by asking directly for their vote.

Can you see how asking people for a referral is like asking them to vote for you?

So make sure they're willing to introduce people to you first.

Here's one way you can say it:

"In the event that you do come across someone, I'm wondering if it would be okay for us to talk about the best way to introduce him or her to me."

Here's what I'm NOT saying:

"The best way would be to introduce us..."

I'm not asking to be introduced, I'm asking about the best way to be introduced. Can you see the difference?

Whenever you ask for that little agreement in advance to a future behavior and they say yes, the likelihood of them keeping that agreement is much higher.

So when you say, *"I'm curious. If you feel comfortable with the way that I work with you, would that mean you would be comfortable introducing me to your family, your friends and your neighbors sometime in the future?"*

And when they say, *"Yes, I'd be comfortable doing that,"* they've made an agreement which makes it easier for you to ask in the future.

How to Discover Who's MOST LIKELY to Refer Others to You

Many years ago when I wrote the workbook for the Main Event program, I listed the criteria for those clients and associates who could become advocates for you and your business. These same characteristics can also be found in those who make great referrals.

But there's one element that's far more important than any other...

They know a hundred or more people.

But how do you know how many people your clients are in touch with? Here's what you can ask to find out...

"During the holiday season, how many greeting cards do you send out in the mail?"

If the response is that they don't even send cards out, then they don't really have a center of influence that they stay in contact with consistently and predictably.

But what do you think it means if they tell you they send hundreds of Christmas cards every year?

It means they have a database of names, addresses and phone numbers of people they stay in communication with.

Here's another way to find out.

Ask them if they are in contact with people who belong to two or more special interest groups, networks or social organizations.

Research shows that the best person to be an advocate for you is the person who is responsible for a non-profit charitable organization. People who run non-profit organizations have a life that is about introducing people and being connected to people of influence. Their job is to connect people that have resources to help their charitable organizations.

So one of the things I would really encourage you to do is to look for people who are responsible for being around, or who are heads of, charitable or non-profit organizations.

What other kinds of people are most likely to refer other high quality prospects to you?

Someone who works in a business environment where there are a lot of interpersonal contacts, like a dentist.

Who's not a great person to look to for referrals?

Those who are on the computer all day long who only talk to the 12 or so people in their cubicle area all year. They're not great sources of business because they don't mix with a lot of people.

Here's another important thing to look for...

They should be willing to take a risk and refer others, because there *is* a certain inherent risk in introducing people or referring people to others.

They should also be energized by connecting people. For example, I get my haircut in a little salon down the street called Lemongrass, and the young lady who cuts my hair is energized by the thought that she can connect me with all the different people that she knows.

She'll say, *"Oh, you need to go to this restaurant,"* or *"Hey, did you see this movie?"* Sometimes I'll walk in and she'll go, *"Oh, I got a book for you."* She's just inherently energized by connecting people.

There's a restaurant called Chevys. When Chevys opens up a new location, one of their strategies is to invite 100 hairdressers for a free lunch, then give them each five certificates for a free lunch that they can give to other people.

Chevys launches a successful restaurant every time. They use hairdressers because people in that profession are more often connectors and mavens than in many other professions.

So notice in your top 150 people...

- Are there people in charitable organizations?
- Are there people in businesses that have interpersonal connections?
- Are there people who are active mavens?
- Are there people who are energized by connecting people?
- Are there people who are willing to take a risk and endorse people?

These are the types of people you should ask to introduce you to others because they have a certain quality that makes it a lot easier. It's more natural for them to become active introducers for you.

***Amplifier 1* – 3 Clubs**
To see the video training in the
Magic Words Dojo for this dialogue, go to:
www.byreferralonly.com/Amplifier1
(you will need to be logged in)

Amplifier 2

Instead of Using the Word "Service" Use the Word "Help"

You may or may not know that service is a wimpy word.

It's ambiguous.

"Help" on the other hand, indicates someone is in trouble and they need you. Every time you're about to say the word service, stop and think about how you can say the same thing using the word help.

One of the most famous commercials of all time was an ad that first appeared in Time Magazine 50 years ago. In it, a woman is on the ground reaching for a first alert button saying: *"Help. I've fallen and I can't get up."* The phrase has become common in our usage today in many contexts, because help gets our attention.

Here's an example:

"My purpose is for you to be so outrageously happy with the help I give you that you would gladly introduce me to two people you really care about before I even sell your home/help you buy a home/close your loan."

What do you get when you type the world "help" into Google?

The result that comes up most often at the top of the search results is the Beatles' song: *"Help. I need somebody. "*

There are only about 75 words in the entire song, but it uses the word help 17 times.

It's a very powerful song. I encourage you to listen to it and even have it playing in the car while you're working with buyers.

Here's the thing about that song…

It's hypnotic. In fact if you listen to almost all the Beatles songs, they use invisible words, or trance language.

Language like, "I want to hold your hand." This kind of hypnotic language forces you to have to create a picture of whose hand are you holding.

Think about the phrases "help you sell" versus "assist to sell." Assist to sell means I'll be there with you. That's OK, but *help* means you're in trouble and I'm going to help you get out of trouble. It's very powerful when you see what one word can do.

When you're asking for help, just know that underneath, there's a lot of emotion packed into that word *help*, as opposed to the word *service* which doesn't have any of that meaning.

If you look up the word "service," you discover it's a monastic word, meaning unconditional devotion to God. The word has no teeth to it when you want people to notice you, think of you, and then introduce you.

There's got to be more emotion than using the word *service*.

When you start to use the word *help*, you're talking about an experience people are having. When you're talking about *service*, you're saying: *"What do you charge for that?"*

People don't say *"What do you charge for your help?"* They don't say that. That's not part of their consciousness.

Here's Why Asking for Help Is So Critical to the Success of Your Business…

Think about the consequences of not asking for help in your business. If you don't ask for help, you have to chase business.

How many of you would rather stand in a cold shower and rip up $10.00 bills than make cold calls? By not reaching out and asking for help from people you know, you have to pursue people, rather than getting help.

Remember, asking for help when you need it or when you want it is part of being responsible to yourself. Not asking for help is actually making yourself a victim, because you're now waiting for people to reach out and offer to help you first.

When you ask for help you take responsibility. When you don't ask for help you become a victim.

Why do people respond to the word *help*?

People feel upset when they see a person in need. They become motivated to do something to reduce the unpleasant feeling they're having when they're seeing somebody who needs help.

When there's a clear need that someone needs help, people are more likely to help. It's got to be a clear need like: "*Help. I'm falling. I can't get up.*"

It's interesting that when there are large groups of people around and no one is naturally helping a person, it becomes even less likely that someone will step up to help.

You might have heard how in New York City they have muggings where large groups of people witness it and no one helps. There's lot of good evidence that says as soon as one person starts to help, others follow—but one person has to step in and get it started.

The bottom line is this....

People help when they see other people helping. So here's how you can use this in Referral Mastery:

"A friend of mine, John, helped one of his friends by introducing his good co-worker to me. I was able to help him and maybe I could help your friends the way I was able to help John's friend."

If you can talk about how you've helped other people, it's easier for people to offer you their friends to help.

Does this make sense to you? This is all happening at an unconscious level around the word *help*.

Helpfulness is seen in those who have empathy for others. When you describe somebody with empathy you say something like:

"The next time you're in a conversation with somebody who really needs some help…they're struggling to get their home sold, they're upset and they're frustrated, they're aggravated and they really don't know who to turn to for help…"

Now you're putting somebody into a role where they become empathetic and altruistic, and they want to help because they're called upon.

Here's what you DON'T want to say:

"The next time you notice somebody who needs to reset their mortgage because their interest rate is too high…"

Can you see how there isn't enough empathy in this statement?

If you can give people the sense they are helping someone who's almost a victim, you'll access their empathy:

"Hey, the next time you're in a conversation with a person who wants to buy their first home and you're a little concerned that they might get advice that might not be in their best interest or they end up with a mortgage payment that's so much higher than what they could've gotten if they had the

right advice or end up paying tens of thousands of dollars more than what they should've, then may even lose their house because they didn't get the right advice, would you think of me and call me immediately so I can give them the help *that they need?"*

The 7 "Magic" Words You Can Use to Make Anyone Pay Attention to You INSTANTLY

I call these implosion words because once someone hears them everything else they are thinking comes to a stop.

Once your client hears one of these words, their mind stops and waits for what comes next. Help is one of these words.

When you say help the mind stops and is thinking: *"Help who? Help what? What do you mean help?"* There's a place in the mind that just pauses for a minute.

Here are the other implosion words: now, secret, stop, imagine, new, next and—of course—sex!

If you go to Barnes & Noble and look at all the magazines, these seven words appear more frequently than any other words on the covers of magazines like Glamour, GQ, Oprah, etc.

Take those seven words and count how many times they appear.

Why do these magazines use them?

Because they get you to stop whatever else you're doing and open the magazine!

These words cause an implosion in your mind. They make you stop and want to know what they're talking about.

Are There Really Such Things as Invisible Words? YES! And Here's Why You Need to Know about Them…

Can you name the most commonly used word in all of the English language? It is a word that holds no meaning by itself. And after that, can you name the next nine most commonly used words?

Here's a hint: I've just said all 10.

Those words are:

1. the
2. of
3. to
4. and
5. a
6. in
7. is
8. it
9. you
10. that

What's important about knowing these top 10 words?

Only one of those words actually carries a picture everyone can agree on. The rest of them are invisible words, meaning when you say the word there is no picture that we agree on. These are not the only invisible words, as you'll see later. But these are a special kind of invisible word.

When I say "it," you have a particular *it* in mind, and I have a different *it* in mind. The only word that we agree has a specific picture is *you*. The rest are invisible words.

It's interesting that when you take out the invisible words, language patterns appear more intellectual—you seem to go from a third grade level to a doctorate degree.

People who speak this way are unconsciously removing invisible words. That makes them harder to understand, because they've removed the mortar between words. Invisible words are the mortar that provides little bits of context to help us comprehend how ideas string together.

Notice all the invisible language—these words as well as others—throughout all the dialogues I'm giving you, and you'll also see the *implosion* words embedded inside all those Magic Words cards.

***Amplifier 2* – A Hearts**
To see the video training in the
Magic Words Dojo for this dialogue, go to:
www.byreferralonly.com/Amplifier2
(you will need to be logged in)

Amplifier 3

Stop Trying to Satisfy Clients and Make Them Happy Instead

This may come as a surprise to you.

All the research I've done around "satisfied customers" shows that this phrase is really a myth!

How is this possible? Isn't this what every business is after?

You see the problem is that satisfaction is already a prerequisite for someone to introduce or refer someone to you!

No one will introduce or refer anyone to you if they're not satisfied. And even if they are satisfied it doesn't mean they're going to introduce you to the people they care about most.

Just think about this for a moment...

Do you refer a meal, a movie, or a book just because you're satisfied with it? We don't go out of our way to make a referral simply when we have a satisfactory experience.

That's because satisfaction is a minimum expectation. Satisfaction only reduces the negative word of mouth; it doesn't increase the positive word of mouth.

One of my favorite books is called the *Ultimate Question* by Fred Reichheld. Fred has been practicing the ultimate question with Fortune 500 companies for the last 20 years, and he believes that it's the only question you'll ever need to ask to determine if a person is happy with what you have done for them.

The ultimate question is...

How likely is it that you will recommend this company to a friend or colleague?

Fred rates answers on a scale of zero to 10 and puts the answers into categories. Someone who scores between a nine and a 10 is a "promoter." A passive person who is satisfied will score between seven and eight. A "detractor" will score between zero and six.

A score of more than half the scale is a detractor!

So if you were to ask your buyers, sellers, and borrowers: *"How likely is it that you would recommend my company to a friend or a colleague, with 10 high and one low?"* what would their response be? What about if you asked the same question every year?

You want to find out your net promotion score: the number of promoters minus the number of detractors (promoters – detractors = net promotion score). There are only two or three companies in the entire country that score in the nine or 10 range.

One of the highest is Harley-Davidson. Harley-Davidson has an almost cult-like following. People are highly active loyalists for that company. Apple is another that's high. Dell is an example of one that's low. You'll find wherever there's almost a cult-like following, the company will have a really high net promotion score.

So what Reichheld's *ultimate question* helps you see is that a "satisfied" client is really a passive person who can be wooed away by the competitors.

If you're scoring anything below a nine, you're working with a satisfied client, and it's your responsibility to keep adjusting all your services with them until they turn into a promoter who enthusiastically goes out and advocates for you.

We've been using the promotion score at our company for the last three years, and our net promotion score right now is a nine. When we first started scoring, we were a seven. Then at every meeting we looked at that score first to see how many people were truly promoters for us, how many were satisfied or passive, and how many of them were detractors. We then made adjustments every month.

How do we do that?

First, we look at what all the detractors are saying and what their comments are, and then we look at what all the satisfied people are saying, and finally what all the promoters are saying. We then make adjustments accordingly.

"What can we do to take it up a tenth of a point?" Our intention is to get our 9 up to a 9.5 or a 10. We want everybody to be a promoter.

Why not do the same for your business? You aren't looking for satisfied customers, but promoters—people who are enthusiastically, energetically, happily, outrageously advocating for you.

It's a very powerful concept to move away from the word satisfied and engage only in the word happy.

***Amplifier 3* – A Clubs**
To see the video training in the
Magic Words Dojo for this dialogue, go to:
www.byreferralonly.com/Amplifier3
(you will need to be logged in)

Amplifier 4

Use the Word "Family" to Create an Automatic Trust with Your Clients

How quickly can you use a single "Magic Word" to create unconscious trust with your clients?

The answer may surprise you!

The book *The Cultural Code* by Clotaire Rapaille is a study of advertising in America written by a gentleman who wrote most of the advertising campaigns for the big Fortune 500 companies.

The cultural code in America around a bathroom is very different than in European countries.

Stay with me here.

You can see by the size of the bathroom what the bathroom represents. In new homes today, the bathroom is a place to have privacy, to escape, to get away. In European cultures, the bathroom is a place to get in and get out.

In the USA when they market products that go in the bathroom, it's a very personal experience because the code is that the bathroom is a private experience where you feel good. It's rooted in our childhood when we would go to the bathroom without mommy's help and we would get lots of praise. It has to do with the code in our culture.

The study in *The Culture Code* looks at many products and services that are sold by large companies who use similar codes rooted in our culture. One of the neat things I thought was the way they put the whole McDonalds campaign together using the words, "You're going to love it," because fast-food is permission to escape.

The code is that you get lost in your hamburger. You get to disappear and you're going to love it. They've learned that whenever they can put the culture code inside of their message it builds unconscious trust with the client.

The author talks about the words "friends, family, and neighbor" as in "Like a good neighbor, State Farm is there." Or "You're in good hands with Allstate." These words embed the word "trust."

If you put the word friend before what you're going to say, it's like embedding the word trust without saying the word specifically.

Here's an example:

"I'm going to give you the same advice I'd give a good friend. If you are my friend, here is what I would suggest that you do, based on your circumstances."

Another way to say it is: *"This is what I'd say to my best friend."*

You can use the words family and neighbor in the same way. You might say to a person...

"If you were my daughter or anyone in my family, here is what I would suggest that you do."

Can you see how different this is from...

"As your mortgage broker, here is what I'd suggest that you do."

The words mortgage broker don't carry the trust code with it, whereas family, friends, and neighbors do.

Now for something even more fascinating.

What if you could create a mnemonic out of the word "family" and spell it out in a way to your clients that helped create trust? Here's what I mean:

"The first thing that we do is we first analyze all of your needs."

Then write down the letter F.

Next, write down the letter A.

"Then we actively go out and find you a loan."

Write down the letter M.

"We meet all the contractual agreements."

Now the letter I.

"We integrate all the work and initiate a settlement date."

The letter L.

"Let's all come together and celebrate your new home and you."

Finally, write down the letter Y.

"Why? Because you now live together as a family in your new home."

Now the word FAMILY is spelled out on your paper. All you want people to remember is the good feeling associated with what you do, not all of the things that you do.

You could take any word and do the same thing, devising your own language to go with each letter of the word you want to convey.

This process is called morphing.

It's a technique where clients will only remember the one word, but all the feelings you described are also embedded in the word.

I love the idea of using the word family when you're talking about a loan, family when you're talking about a home, and family when you're talking about moving.

Because that's what it all comes down to—the trust that you're going to take care of your client's family.

***Amplifier 4* – 6 Hearts**
To see the video training in the
Magic Words Dojo for this dialogue, go to:
www.byreferralonly.com/Amplifier4
(you will need to be logged in)

Amplifier 5:

Have Clients Call You "Friend" as Quickly as Possible

Much like the word family, the word friend can carry a lot of power to get referrals. Here's an example of how you can use it:

"Isn't it nice to know you have a friend in the business that you are comfortable referring the people you care about to?"

Here are a few other examples:

"It's good to have a friend in the business, isn't it?"

"You might become aware of how good you feel when you let the other agent know that you have a friend in the business."

You can sign all of your letters, *Your Friend in the Real Estate Business.*

The reason I love that word friend is because it is the way people refer you. They say *"I have a friend in the business."* When a person's going to advise another person they care about to use you as a real estate or a mortgage consultant they say, *"Hey, you ought to call my friend. He's in the real estate business."*

But here's a mistake I see all the time.

We tend to refer to ourselves as a real estate consultant even when the client is referring to us as a friend.

Start by identifying yourself as their friend.

The faster we can get a person to use the word friend in identifying us, the better.

I love the whole notion of saying to people, *"Well let me give you the advice a good friend would give another good friend."*

Here's what to say if someone asks you what you think their house is worth.

"Well, I'd suggest the same thing I would suggest to a really good friend."

Isn't advice that comes from a friend different than advice coming from a real estate consultant?

Of course it is! And the more you continually refer to yourself as their friend, the more they'll associate you with friendship.

"Isn't it nice to know you have a friend in the business you can trust and that you can feel real comfortable introducing the people that you care about most to? Isn't that a nice thing?"

Here's the thing. Most people want to have a friend in the business. They want a friend they can refer others to so they can be the hero for their friends.

How many times have you thought the following:

"Boy, I wish I had a friend who was a plumber."

Over time I've noticed that the girl who cuts my hair has become a friend. The same with my therapist and life coach. And when I refer to Amy, my acupuncturist/masseuse, I say, *"Oh, you need to see my friend, Amy. She really does a great job as a masseuse."*

There's something that happens when you cross over that line and start to call someone a friend. It's no longer about price. It's no longer about trust. It's about the relationship. And once you cross over, it's hard to go back to calling someone just your real estate agent or carpet cleaner.

Be more aggressive in referring to yourself as their friend, as opposed to waiting for them to call you their friend.

Here's how you can start:

After somebody lists or buys your property or decides to work with you, you can say to them:

"You're going to be out looking at homes and you're going to run across other real estate agents. To make everyone feel comfortable, say to all the other real estate agents that you already have a friend in the business."

Just think about how discouraging it is when somebody says they already have a friend in the business. You feel like you have no shot. So you want your friends and clients to say that to other agents about you.

Whenever you're sending people to look at open houses, ask them to walk in, show the listing agent your card and tell the agent, *"I already have a friend in the business."*

It's not *"I know an agent"* which is different than *"I have a friend in the business."*

There's more strength around the word friend.

***Amplifier 5* – 7 Hearts**
To see the video training in the
Magic Words Dojo for this dialogue, go to:
www.byreferralonly.com/Amplifier5
(you will need to be logged in)

Amplifier 6

Turn into Someone Your Clients Already Like!

Here's a popular slogan you're probably familiar with:

"Like a good neighbor, State Farm is there."

The idea is that a good neighbor is someone you can trust, who's courteous and friendly, and always there for you when you need them.

A neighbor is a source of help when you are in trouble. Someone you can count on. Somebody who cares about you. If you have a good neighbor, you know that if anything ever happened you could always turn to them for help.

In most communities, there is at least the notion of a neighbor as being a friend. The word neighbor morphs between someone who lives nearby to friend.

Take a look at www.morphthing.com. It takes the pictures of two people and morphs them together to see what they would look like if they were combined. So it takes John Travolta and Oprah Winfrey or Bill Clinton and Muhammad Ali and puts their faces together. You can upload your picture into it and morph it with any other picture you want.

If you can morph yourself into being seen as a client's neighbor, then they will also consider you a friend and make it more likely to say yes to refer you.

Here's how you can do that.

When you say things like, *"Imagine I'm like a good neighbor,"* what you're actually doing is morphing a good neighbor they have in their mind onto you and blending you and them into one. You don't have to know who their good neighbor is. When you say the word *neighbor* their unconscious mind fills in the picture.

So when you say, *"Isn't it nice to know that, like a good neighbor, I'm always here?"* the unconscious mind finds the picture of the good neighbor and morphs it with you, which creates a good feeling. Just use the word *neighbor* and the unconscious mind does the rest of the work.

Remember the most important part of generating a referral or getting an introduction is helping people feel good about you.

Using the word neighbor in this way follows the principles that Dr. Cialdini lays out in his book the *Six Principles of Influence*. One of the principles is called "liking."

People prefer to say "yes" to people they know and like. If you like your neighbor, you associate neighborliness with liking.

And if you like me, it's easier for you to say *yes* to me. If I can morph the word neighbor onto me, it's easier for you to say yes to me because you're saying *yes* to somebody who is like a neighbor...who you already like.

If someone thinks of you as their neighbor, they are more willing to say *yes* to a request without a lot of consideration.

Imagine if a neighbor says, *"Could I borrow a cup of sugar?"*

Do you ask: *"Well, when are you going to give it back to me?"* Of course not.

Here are a few more ways to morph yourself into a neighbor.

"I'm going to give to you the same advice that a good neighbor would give you."

"Remember, if you list your home with me, it's like listing it with a good neighbor. I'm going to see you all the time."

When you use those words to identify yourself, it's easier for people to say *yes* without thinking... *"First, let me see your resume. Let me talk to people you've worked with in the past."*

Why not? Because that's not what they would say to a neighbor.

They don't say to a neighbor, *"Well, who else have you borrowed sugar from that you've given the sugar back that I could talk to?"*

The word neighbor eliminates a lot of that.

How to Increase Your Familiarity So Clients See You as Their Neighbor

The more contact that you have with the person in a favorable location, the more they will see you as a neighbor.

The more they see you in happy circumstances, like at weddings or barbeques, baptisms, and at the grocery store, the more they see you as a neighbor—even if you don't live nearby.

Can you see the direct correlation?

When clients come in contact with you in the kinds of environments where they might run into their neighbors, the more they will identify you as a neighbor instead of a real estate agent or lender.

You may not live in their neighborhood, but if they are familiar with you in their neighborhood at events or situations where they see other neighbors, then a very powerful principle says: *"If I see you there, I like you because you're just like me."*

Dr. Cialdini did a neat study in which researchers went into an upscale neighborhood—I mean behind the gated entry and manicured lawns, giant homes and guards—and they asked residents if they could put a big 7 x 7 sign in their lawn. They said they'd drill holes into the lawn and the sign would say: *"Please drive safely for the sake of the children."*

They went from door to door and found only 17% were willing to put that sign in their lawn. Then they went back and asked the people to put a small sign, just like an 8.5" x 11" sign, in their window saying the same thing. 86% of the people were willing to put the smaller sign in their window.

Then they went back six weeks later and asked the people who put the sign in their window if they were now willing to put the sign in their lawn and they found there was a 70% increase of those willing to put the sign in the lawn.

There's something very powerful about this idea—when somebody becomes familiar with something, when they start to see it regularly, like when you are around more and your mailings and communications are around more—they become willing to make bigger commitments.

Neighbor assumes they are already familiar with us. It assumes we are already in their lives. And when you refer to yourself as a good neighbor throughout your communication, it's like you blend into their lives.

When you ask someone to make a commitment like *"list your home with me," "buy a home with me," "do a loan from me,"* it's hard to turn around and do it with a stranger—a lender or realtor they're meeting for the first time.

But when you show up as a neighbor, refer to yourself as a neighbor, it's easier for them to make a bigger commitment.

***Amplifier* 6 – 8 Hearts**
To see the video training in the
Magic Words Dojo for this dialogue, go to:
www.byreferralonly.com/Amplifier6
(you will need to be logged in)

Amplifier 7

10 "Invisible" Words You Can Use to Become an Incredible Communicator

When you study great hypnotic communicators, 10 words keep appearing over and over again in the phrases they use. I call them "invisible" words because we don't pay much attention to them consciously when we hear them, but our unconscious is very aware of how powerful they are.

These are different from the kind of invisible words that are the most common words in the English language. These are hypnotic invisible words.

As you go through all of the dialogues in the Referral Mastery Program you're going to become aware of these words.

You can use these words to help you remember the dialogues by using them to break up what you need to memorize...moving from invisible word to invisible word.

And when you read the dialogues and take the invisible words out you'll see the meaning of the sentence totally changes.

1. Invisible Word: "Because"

"When a family member, friend, or neighbor needs advice about buying, selling, or borrowing, please don't keep me a secret **because** you want them to get the best possible results and be delighted that you introduced me, don't you?"

When I was about 16 years old curfew at my house was 10:00 pm.

"Hey, Mom, can I stay out till 10:30?"

"No, you be home by 10:00."

"Come on, Mom."

"Young man, you be home at 10:00."

What would have happened if I knew at 16 what I know today? What would have I said to my mom?"

"Mom, can I stay out until 10:30 this one time ***because*** *we're going over to Bill's house to watch a movie and* ***because*** *the movie is over at 10:00 and* ***because*** *it takes 30 minutes to get home from Bill's? Would you* ***be kind*** *enough to* ***trust me*** *this one time and I'll be home by 10:30?"*

When you use the word "because" it makes everything after it three to five times stronger. So when you say...

"Please don't keep me a secret because..." and then give the reason why, it makes what you're asking for three to five times stronger.

Ellen Langer did research on people standing in front of a Xerox machine at Harvard University. She had people walk up and say, *"Could I cut in line?"*

Four out of ten people (40%) would let them.

Then she had them add the word because along with a brief explanation: *"Could I cut in line* ***because*** *I'm late for class?"*

94% of the people in line would let them, just by adding the word because with a short explanation.

Here are a few more ways to create more agreement:

"I want to meet with you today ***because*** *I know I can help you sell your home."*

"I want you to refer me to the people that you care about ***because*** *they deserve to get the best advice possible when it's time for them to make a decision who to use."*

"I want you to introduce me to the people in your office ***because*** *when you're in an environment with like-minded agents or lenders, your production improves."*

One of the most important characteristics of a compelling argument is **because** the word "because" is the most effective word to give a reason why.

We just want to know, *"Why should I do this?"*

"Because" answers all of the "why's."

2. Invisible Word: "But"

Imagine the word "but" as a U-turn sign.

When people are telling you where they want to go and they put a "but" in front of it, it takes them completely in another direction.

Whenever we use the word "but" we're negating what they hear. Most people are very sensitive to this word so use it diligently and properly.

Here are some effective ways to use "but" without negating the feelings people have.

Let's say someone says to you, "Joe, I'd really love to come to the Magic Words workshop, **but** I'm really busy."

What's the last feeling you are left with?

"Oh, you're too busy to do that."

Here's a way to repeat the original sentence back to them while flipping the ideas around using "but."

"Oh, so you're really busy, ***but*** *you'd love to come to the Magic Words Workshop."*

You hear the flip?

Now try it yourself. Flip the following statement:

"I want to buy a home, ***but*** *I don't have the money."*

Becomes…

"You don't have the money, ***but*** *you want to buy a home."*

You might even add another sentence.

"You don't have the money, ***but*** *you want to buy a home. I'm wondering, what would have to happen for you to buy that home?"* Leaving them with that last thought of "buy the home" lets you lock it down for them.

Or you might just say *"imagine that."*

"So what I hear you saying is that you don't have the money, but you'd really like to buy a home? Well, imagine that."

They're imagining they don't have the money…what you're suggesting is that they imagine buying the house.

How to Negate a Positive with an Even GREATER Positive

Even though "but" is a negating word, you can negate a positive with an even greater positive.

If you're putting up ugly yellow signs and you're recording the scripts to my phone leads, one of the lines at the end of the script sounds like this:

"There's just too much to tell you about in this brief recorded message, ***but*** *it's easy for you to get more information. Just leave me a message."*

It's really two great things. It's a negation of a positive by a greater positive. The "but" erases the thought of getting more information and leaves them with the thought of *"Call me."*

When you hear the word "but," notice if it is erasing the good…what they want or erasing the bad…what they don't want. Flip it so it's erasing the bad and ending on the good.

Werner Erhard said, "Everything before ***but*** is bull."

Negative self-talk is an example. If you're having a conversation with yourself and you notice yourself saying something like, *"This is going to be really hard,"* just add "but" and then say something positive: "… ***but** I can learn this quickly."*

3. Invisible Word: "And"

"And" is a great connecting word.

"And" is going to connect multiple thoughts together. the more thoughts you connect with "and," the embedded command or thought at the end of your sentence is going to become stronger.

*"You may be wondering how you can own a home of your own **and** stop paying rent **and** start creating equity **and** how you can do that now."*

When you're with a client and you want to use "and" to recap what's happened in the day, recall what happened and say:

*"Yesterday when we talked on the phone **and** decided to meet this morning to find your dream home **and** discover what you like **and** what you don't like, you said when you saw the right home you would know **and** you would tell me. Now that we've met **and** looked at seven houses I'm curious, do you **feel close to your dream home?"***

Notice each "and" drops them deeper?

You're building a story more and more deeply with everything you link together. *"And do you feel close to your dream home?"* is the embedded command *"Feel close to your dream home."*

It's the "ands" that build evidence.

One of the things you may notice is that people will string "ands" together as they're telling a story, a story they haven't thought out and you're falling deeper and deeper into the story and you don't **want to**!

4. Invisible Word: "Yet"

When someone calls you and they want to break an appointment with you and they say:

*"Hey, Joe, I'm sorry. I know I cancelled our last loan appointment **and** I believe I may need to cancel tonight. I have some problems here at work **and** I have a shipment that hasn't arrived yet **and** two people who can fix it are out sick today **and** I'm not clear how today will pan out."*

So they strung together their story with the people who were sick and the shipment that's not there and they don't believe that they can do it.

A response to help them very compassionately through that would be:

*"John, I've always told you I have time for you, your family and your colleagues who you care about **and** I appreciate your schedule **and** of course we can change **and** I hear you have a lot happening today **yet** you want to be clear what's important about being here to you."*

The "yet" takes almost everything they said and ignores almost all of it to focus on: *"**Yet** there's something else that you want."*

For example if you say to me:

"Well, I just don't know how to learn these dialogues!"

All I need to say to that is "yet!"

The "yet" erases everything and pulls you all the way through the story.

It's a great thing when somebody says "I don't have any money to buy a home" and you say ***"Yet**."*

"It doesn't mean you won't, just right now you don't."

"Yet" gets them off of that position and lets them start to invent ways to move forward.

5. Invisible Word: "Try"

"Try" is a funny word because when we hear people use the word "try" we know that what they're really saying is, *"I don't believe I can do that."*

"Hey, can you get me those documents by 5:00 tonight?"

*"Yes, I'll **try** to do that!"*

"I'm curious, is there anything you could think of that would stop you from getting that by 5:00 tonight?"

"Well, actually I have to get to the drycleaners by 3:30 and have to get my daughter from the daycare by 4:30 so that maybe a little challenging to do."

Now you can get resourceful.

"Can your assistant get your dry cleaning? Or can you meet at 8 pm?"

What I've learned is when somebody says "try," they're putting their excuse in one word. They have this big story they don't know how to explain so they put it into one word called "try."

Usually it's a story they may be embarrassed about or it's a secret or it's something that they don't want to disclose to you. Or there's a lot going on and they don't want to bother explaining, so the easiest way to handle it is with one word: "try."

*"I'll **try** to make it."*

*"When you say **try**, can you help me better understand that? What are the possibilities that this is going to happen because that **'try'** didn't sound real confident?"*

There are appropriate times to use "try." It's okay for you to say:

"You can try and negotiate this on your own. You can **try** to oversee all these transactional details. You can **try** and ask yourself profound questions. You can **try** that."

Now what you're doing with the word "try" is you're using it to cast doubt. So when somebody says, *"We're going to do this on our own."* You say, *"You can **try** it."*

Here is another great example.

Someone wants to sell their home for $540,000 and you know they can really only get $510,000. I'd want to empathize with them.

*"I appreciate you want to **try** to get $540,000 for your home. If I were in your shoes, I'd want to **try** that too. Let me tell you what Larry Johnson **tried**."*

Then you can tell the story of Larry Johnson who got an offer for $599,000, but tried to get $610,000. He later got a much lower offer.

"Try" implies failure. "*We **tried** that and then we **tried** this and we **tried** that.*" "Try" weakens everything after it and you can use that.

6. Invisible Word: "If"

"If" is the same as imagine.

When you say to someone, *"**If** you owned a home,"* it's the same as *"Imagine you own a home"* because "if" has to presuppose something like imagine does.

When people put an identity label on themselves such as "I can't do that," it's really that they *believe* they can't do that. It's hard for them to move away from "I can't do that. That's not possible for me."

You can use an "if" pattern to help them move beyond that position:

"I really can't afford to make that house payment."

*"Well, what would happen **if** you could make that house payment?"*

So when somebody says to me, *"I'm frustrated,"* they've labeled themselves. It's like labeling yourself by saying *"I'm a golfer," "I'm a hockey player," "I'm a gardener," "I'm frustrated," "I'm a Realtor."*

Now you detach them from that label by saying, *"I understand you feel frustrated. **If** you did buy a home, what would happen?"*

Sometimes people confuse feelings with identity especially when they are under pressure. But you can disconnect them from identifying with the feeling like this:

"I am just sick and tired."

*"So what I hear you saying is you feel sick and tired. **If** you could get an answer by 3:00, what would that feel like?"*

7. Invisible Word: "To"

"To" is a great command because it takes you right to the thing that you want.

When you put the word "to" in front of anything, the very next thing that you say is going to be directly what they want. There's no other direction. It's also going to be in the present tense and it's going to be a command.

For example:

"You buy a house ***to*** *create an environment for your family and* ***to create wealth*** *with real estate and* ***to*** *live in a place that you're proud of* ***to*** *really experience the American Dream."*

When you lower your voice when you say *"to create wealth"* that's really what embeds that command deeply for people. You're using the word "to" in place of "and."

8. Invisible Word: "When"

"When" is great. "When" is a time machine. "When" will take you from wherever you are right now to where you want to be.

"So ***when*** *you walk in the home that you're looking for, what will you see?" "****When*** *you are in your dream home what will you hear? " "Imagine what will it feel like* ***when*** *you're in that home?"*

Notice how this moves them towards their goal which is, *"****When*** *I'm in that home."* So really it really is a time machine.

When you work with a client, say this right at the beginning:

"What do you folks want?"

"Well, we're looking for a three-bedroom home."

*"****When*** *you walk into this three-bedroom home, how will you know it's the home for you? What will you feel? What will you see or hear* ***when*** *you walk in and you know it's yours?"*

People have to move mentally there and describe it.

It's important to realize that when people describe what they are seeing they're giving you their *hot words.*

Learn those words, exactly what they're saying.

So when they say, *"Oh, gosh. We would feel a sense of peace,"* here's what you must remember:

"We would feel a sense of peace."

Now when you walk into the house, you say:

*"**When** you are here now are you feeling a sense of peace?"*

The words they say when you ask questions that begin with "when" are giving you the hottest words in the unconscious part of their decision making mind.

9. Invisible Word: "Or"

There are two types of "or."

There's an open "or" and a closed "or."

A *closed or* would be where you offer a limited number of options:

*"Would you like to have a 15-year mortgage **or** a 30-year mortgage?"*

There are really only two places to go with that. A lot of times it helps to bring clarity to people, if that's what they need. But sometimes it may feel like a bit of trap to people.

So that would lead to the other type of "or," which is an *"open or."*

*"Would you like to have a 15-year mortgage **or** another investment opportunity that's going to help you build wealth the way that you want to?"*

Here is another good example:

"Would Monday be good ***or*** *would you rather do it Tuesday?"* That's an appropriate question. But if you want to open it up you say...

"You can do it on Monday ***or*** *whatever day is comfortable with you when you feel like it's the time to discuss selling your home because you know I can get it sold."*

You're putting all of your action in their options. Watch people say, *"Well, that would be Thursday then!"*

10. Invisible Word: "So"

"So" is nice because you get to forget what came before and move towards something better.

I have found myself naturally doing that in a lot of my recordings where I will start out with "***So****, here's what I want to talk to you about next..."* or *"****So*** *that means..."* and it kind of weaves things together in an invisible, seamless way.

***Amplifier* 7 – 2 Spades**
To see the video training in the
Magic Words Dojo for this dialogue, go to:
www.byreferralonly.com/Amplifier7
(you will need to be logged in)

Amplifier 8

Use Client Hot Words to Get More Introductions and Look More Professional

When you ask people to share with you what is important to them, you may hear people use words like "trust", "integrity," "great service," or "value."

The exact words they use are called *hot words*. Here's why hot words are so important:

You can use them to have tremendous influence with clients. The secret is you have to use their exact words, not your interpretation of the words—their *exact* words.

A nice dialogue to discover hot words around introducing people would be:

"I'm curious to know what's important to you when you refer your family or friend or a neighbor to a real estate or mortgage consultant."

Listen to their answer for the exact words they use. These are the words you say back to them when talking about referring you.

"What's important to you when you refer a family, a friend, or a neighbor to a real estate consultant?"

"Well, that person does what they say they're going to do."

"So what I hear you're saying is when you refer me, you want me to do what I say I'm going to do."

Can you see how this changes it from referring a real estate consultant to using their own words?

"So what I hear you saying is that you want me to do what I say."

"Yes, that's what I want you to do."

Then in the future you would remember to say:

"Casey, thanks for introducing me to the people that you care about. Remember, I will do what I say I will do."

So I'm using Casey's hot words again.

When you're going into a relationship, people have certain hot words that carry a lot of importance to them. Make a mental note of what they are.

You can even put the words that are important to them on your little yellow sticky pad on your customer experience timeline.

Out of the entire range of words they could've picked, they picked those words, so give them back to them exactly the same way and they will associate you with that idea.

Here's an Important Pattern You Need to Be Aware of...

Wyatt Woodsmall wrote a brilliant book called *People Pattern Power.* It's a pretty complex integration of a lot of NLP and hypnosis, but there's one particular pattern that I listen for a lot.

It's called "the sameness and the difference pattern."

Some people will respond with the sameness pattern, meaning they'll say something like: *"Well, I want you to give the same experience that you gave me."* They'll use the same terms to describe something they have experienced that they want others to experience.

A different pattern experience will be: *"Well, you'll have to ask them and find out what they want."* They'll say something different than what they've experienced. They have a totally different way of referring. So just notice the patterns.

Some people use sameness with a qualifier. They'll say something like, *"Well, do the same thing you did for them, but make sure you ask them if that's important to them too."*

Some people say a difference with a qualifier. They'll say, *"Well, you'll ask them what they want and then make sure you do what they say they're going to do."*

What Will that Do for You?

Another pattern that you want to notice is when you ask this question...

"What will that do for you?"

For example...

"What's important about the qualities in a real estate agent or a lender when you refer them to a friend or a family member?"

"Well, I really want them to have integrity and I want them to be really honest and I want them to do the same thing that they did for me."

"So what I hear you saying is you want me to be honest, you want me to have integrity and you want me to do the same thing I did for you?"

"Yes, that's what I want."

"What would that do for you?"

See if they answer with something that moves them **away from what they want to avoid** or moves them **closer towards what they want**.

They are moving towards something when they answer with something like:

"Well, that would encourage me to want to refer more people to you."

If they use a negative to describe what something would do for them, they are moving away from what they don't want. Like this:

"Well, that would make sure I don't make a mistake."

When you're doing the 5-6-7 you can say*: "So what's important about buying a home for you?"*

"Well, we get a much larger house."

"What would that do for you?"

"We wouldn't be in such a cramped room." They're talking about what they don't want versus what they do want.

Here's another example of moving towards what they want:

"What would that do for you?"

"It gives us a bigger backyard and more room to play."

Moving away from what they don't want sounds like:

"What would that do for you?" "

"Well, the kids wouldn't have such a small yard to play in and they wouldn't be so cramped back there."

Here's the secret to maximizing your influence…

Match their patterns. When they're moving away, you start moving away with them.

"Oh, so what I understand is what you don't want is a small cramped backyard."

Imagine that with them. Imagine being in a small cramped backyard and what that feels like.

Here's what NOT to say:

"Oh, well, imagine having a big backyard."

Why? Because they're moving AWAY from small yard, not moving TOWARDS a big yard. Does that make sense to you? When you're listening for what's important to them, be listening to the pattern.

Is it important for them to be the same or to be different? Is it important for them to move away from what they don't want? Or is it important for them to move towards what they want?

When you find what's hot for them, stay with their pattern as opposed to imposing your pattern on them.

That's what hot words are all about.

***Amplifier 8* – 5 Clubs**
To see the video training in the
Magic Words Dojo for this dialogue, go to:
www.byreferralonly.com/Amplifier8
(you will need to be logged in)

Amplifier 9

Tell People EXACTLY How to Refer Others to You

Now I'm going to tell you how you can get many more introductions...and have far fewer people forget about you!

There are three things you need to get referrals:

1. **People have to notice other people.**

2. **They've got to think of you.**

3. **They've got to introduce you.**

The easiest way to make sure your get all three things is by using the following dialogue:

"Mr. and Mrs. Client, here are three simple steps to follow in the days and weeks ahead when you're in a conversation with a person who mentions they are considering buying or selling a home or getting a loan...

Step one, take out your cell phone. Step two, look up my phone number. Step three, call me immediately...

When we talk, you can tell me what you think would be the best way to get into a conversation with the person you want to introduce to me."

I love this dialogue because it can be used in so many different ways. You can use those three commands, "*Step one, step two, step three,"* as an e-mail signature. Or use them in your newsletter or EOS postcards.

Use these three steps anytime you provide specific instructions on how people can introduce you.

Did You Know There Are 3 Filters People Use To Interpret The Outside World?

Noam Chomsky wrote a book called *Transformational Grammar* in which he says there are three linguistic processes people use to create the "filters" that enable them to interpret their own individual world.

One is called **deletion**. Deletion is a result of the conscious mind only being able to handle seven, plus or minus two, chunks of information simultaneously.

On a good day, you can handle nine things coming at you and on a bad day more like five. So when you say to a person, *"Step one, take out your cell phone. Step two, look up my number. Step three, call me,"* we know the conscious mind can handle that because there is no ambiguity to it at all. There is nothing to be deleted from that message.

But what happens if you say this?

"When you come across somebody who is interested in buying a home, would you let me know?"

A lot of that could be mentally deleted because there is no clarity. There too many components to "let me know." Way more than nine components for the unconscious mind to understand.

But when you break it down into steps it's easier for the conscious mind to store in long-term memory because there is nothing to delete.

Another factor Noam Chomsky talked about was **distortion**.

You know that you've done this, too. Have you ever imagined old furniture in a new room? Your mind is distorting things.

When you suggest to people that they refer you, they create their own organization of information built under their ability to refer you. They distort it.

Here's why this is dangerous. If you're not specific and you say:

"Would you refer me?"

Clients come up with different distortions around what that means. They could think, *"Okay, I'll send them to a main event. Oh, no, no, I'll have them go over to a half day. Or even better yet, why don't I just have them call up one of the coaches? No, I'll just let Joe know next time I see him."*

Without specifics, they distort the word "referral" and create what it means in their own mind. You want to be specific and take away all that ambiguity and allow them not to delete or distort anything.

A third thing Noam Chomsky talked about was **generalization**.

When people lack specificity, they generalize.

I hear this a lot.

"Why don't you go ahead and put up some ugly yellow signs?"

"Well, my broker won't let me do that."

"That's against the rules in my area."

"Our city ordinance says you can't do that."

Can you see how this leads to these real big general statements? Watch what happens instead if I give real simple instructions...

"Okay, so here is what you do. You take a yellow sign. You write the words, 'Free recorded message' and write the

phone number under that and, then you go to a park and right at the intersection across the street from an apartment building you put the sign up."

Speaking specifically, generalizations don't come up.

But when I say, *"Put up ugly yellow signs,"* they get to let their mind go wherever they want it to.

The more specific you are the less likely people are to delete, distort, and generalize what you say.

Here's another example of what this kind of specific dialogue looks like:

"Next time you're in a conversation with a friend, a family member or a neighbor and they mention that they would love to have a larger, more spacious home, perhaps they need to sell their current home and move into a neighborhood that's closer to work.

Maybe it's the cost of gas right now going back and forth and they've talked to you about how painful that is, spending anywhere from $800.00 to $1,000.00 a month in gas and they know if they could move a little closer to work they might be to save $300.00 to $400.00 a month and that could actually be easy for them to do right now.

I know you may come across somebody like that. When you do, would you simply take out your cell phone, look up my number and call me immediately? Then we can get into a conversation and we can talk about the best way you can introduce them to me so I could help them."

***Amplifier 9* – 7 Clubs**
To see the video training in the
Magic Words Dojo for this dialogue, go to:
www.byreferralonly.com/Amplifier9
(you will need to be logged in)

Referral Mastery

37 Exact Ways to Ask for a Referral and Get It Every Time!

<u>**Exact Way to Ask 1**</u>

Print the Right Words on the Back of Your Business Card to DRAMATICALLY Increase Referrals!

When you hand someone your card, you're really providing them with two things.

There's your contact information, which includes your location, address, phone number and email address. The name of your company and your logo puts you into a box called "I'm a realtor."

What appears on the back of your business card is your philosophy. It's what you stand for. **This is the thing you really want to talk about**...not your location or your phone number.

As a matter of fact, it's more important to have them put your phone number into their phone than to give them a card with your phone number because cards get thrown away.

When you're handing somebody your card, you're saying *"If you look on the back...that's what I'm really all about."* Talk about that.

Here are the MAGIC WORDS you can use on the back of your business cards to really increase your referrals.

Imagine me as your real estate or mortgage consultant. What I do for you is invest my time consulting, negotiating, and organizing the details of your transaction because you want to have a superb experience that causes you to want to introduce me to the people that you care about most.

The purpose of my business is referral, which means I must bring value that makes you feel comfortable introducing me to the people you know that need my help. After all, a referral is sending someone you care about to someone you trust.

When you give somebody a card, what you're actually asking them to do is consider you as their real estate consultant.

So when I say *imagine,* they already have to presuppose that you are their real estate consultant. It's self-appointment. Leaders don't say, *"I want to be a real estate consultant."*

The words are: *"Imagine that I am your real estate consultant."*

You're already putting yourself into that role. There's a lot of power in taking the leadership role without asking people to give it to you. If you want them to follow you, then just assume you're already their leader.

Have you noticed most great leaders just assign themselves as leaders?

Let's examine the language pattern closer.

Imagine me as your real estate or mortgage consultant, and what I do for you...

What you do for people is that you invest your time doing three things: consulting, negotiating and overseeing the transactional details.

And the reason you do that is because you want them to have a superb experience that causes them to want to introduce you to the people that you care about most.

That's a great concept to introduce on your business card. It's the concept of **introduce me**.

Then you say...

"Now the purpose of my business (I love that line. I've been using it for years!) *is to bring you enough value that makes* ***you feel comfortable introducing me*** *to the people that you know may need my help."*

Again, the word *help* in this phrase is a powerful suggestion. After all, a referral is sending someone you care about to someone you trust and you want to help those you care about.

So the key words are imagine, consulting, negotiating, organizing the transactional details, because, superb experience, introduce me, the purpose of my business, comfortable introducing me and you trust.

You can use these concepts to build any phrases you want around them.

But I would suggest that these words be **embedded** inside your language, no matter what you choose to put on the back of your business card.

One Simple Phrase That Lets Clients Know Exactly What You Stand for

Perhaps you've already guessed the phrase.

That's right. It's **By Referral Only**.

By properly placing your little gold "By Referral Only" sticker on the front of your business card you're telling people this is your philosophy and what you stand for.

It serves as a "pattern interrupt" that lets you transition into talking about your philosophy.

"On the back of my card is my philosophy and that's what it means."

The word "Only" is very strategic. It causes the mind to say: *"What does that mean?"*

You want people to take you out of the box of a traditional real estate agent or a traditional lender when they look at your card. You want them to look at your card and think, *"What does that mean?"* Then you can show them the back of your card where it explains what it means.

These gold stickers are worth putting on your card.

We license the name to you as a member of By Referral Only. It's a phrase I went through a great deal of time, energy and money to trademark to give you the rights to use and I strongly recommend you do for the value it brings.

My friend Jim McCraig said to me...

"Joe, the program is worth every dime that I spend. Just the words By Referral Only are worth it and if anyone in the (By Referral Only) community decides not to affix it to their business card, they're selling themselves short."

Put it on your card, hand it to people and say: "*See that sticker? It means by referral only and let me explain what that means."* Then flip your card over and have them look at the back. It opens up the dialogue.

***Exact Ways to Ask 1* – 5 Diamonds**
To see the video training in the
Magic Words Dojo for this dialogue, go to:
www.byreferralonly.com/WayToAsk1
(you will need to be logged in)

Exact Way to Ask 2

Use a Voicemail Message to Plant a Referral Seed Fast!

This is a concept we've been teaching for 15 years and I'm always curious when people tell me they already know it.

A student came to his master and said, *"Master, you're teaching me the same thing that you taught me last month."*

"A student who is not practicing what they've already learned has not mastered the art of repetition," replied the master.

What most mediocre students look for is something new. But the master loves the feeling that the soul experiences through the power of repetition.

What do your children say to you when they find a book for the first time and they love it? "Read it again." How many times have you watched Lion King? A child knows they feel more satisfied the more they do something over and over again.

Allow your mind to be fascinated with the *depth* of repetition as opposed to being irritated by the *shallowness* of repetition. The monkey mind has the tendency to say, *"Give me something new. Give me some different idea to work on."*

Tricks to Using Your Voicemail as a Referral Tool

1. You must tell the truth.

Both truth and lies have a frequency that resonates with the heart chakra.

"Your call is really important to me so leave your name and your number and I'll get back to you as soon as possible."

What do you think the person receiving that message is thinking?

"Well, okay. I guess they'll call me back."

Can you see how this would resonate as not true? "As soon as possible" means different things to different people. There's no specificity to it. On the other hand the truth has a lot of accuracy and specificity.

Call yourself what you want others to call you.

When you call yourself an advisor or a consultant, you are giving yourself the title you want others to give to you. Absent of giving yourself a title, they will continue to refer to you as a real estate agent or a mortgage person.

Let people know that you're working.

Not letting them know that you're working means that you're not working. Be specific about what you're doing.

If you're going out on a home inspection and you're going to be gone from 1:00 to 3:00, let people specifically know that you're doing a home inspection.

If you just say, *"I'll be getting back to you as soon as I can,"* without telling them what you're doing, their mind will decide you're doing nothing. In their minds, you're not working.

2. Use future pacing statements as much as possible.

I would love if you could include in each of your voice mail messages something like:

"The next time you're in a conversation, think of me and introduce me."

A good voicemail message might sound like this:

"Hey, thank you for calling. This is Joe Stumpf, your personal real estate/mortgage consultant for life. I'll be back in the office after the inspection that I'll be on and returning phone calls at 1:00 PM. At the sound of the tone please leave your name and your number where I can reach you. And the next time you're in a conversation with a family member or a coworker who mentions that they're currently renting, please picture yourself calling me up and letting me know who they are. I have a great list of homes they can live in for about the same amount of money that they're paying in rent. So, have a great morning. I'll be back at 1:00 PM. Talk to you then."

3. Use the statement "Can you imagine yourself calling?" or "Can you picture a family member?"

It's a rhetorical question that doesn't require a specific answer. But the neat thing is you're having a conversation with their unconscious mind and you're not even present. It's on your voicemail. You're asking them a question they have to answer internally and you're not even there.

Here's what NOT to say:

"Would you please call me if you know anyone."

Instead you'd say…

"Hey, can you imagine yourself calling me when you discover a friend or a family member who needs to buy their first home and telling me who they are?"

4. Always offer something in your voicemail message they can give to a person to help them get what they want.

For example you might say:

"The next time you're in a conversation with a person who mentions they're going to be refinancing from one of those loans that has to be reset in the next couple of months

because their interest rate is going up, can you picture yourself calling and letting me know who they are? I have a list of 10 questions they must ask the next lender before they sign anything. You can call me and I can send you a copy of it to give to your friends. So, have a great morning. I'll be back at 1:00 to return your phone call."

Can you see how this is powerful?

You're asking people to start noticing those who may be resetting their loan. And when they notice them, to think of you.

By providing them with information they can give to someone, you're making them a hero, which makes them more likely to respond.

Every time you ask for an introduction let the person know that you've got something of value to give.

5. Be very specific and congruent with your message.

Your voicemail message should change and be congruent with the messages in your Newsletter, Evidence of Success, and Letter from the Heart.

Suppose this month you're going to ask people to start noticing people who are getting married. You're working with a first time home buyer and you've put a list together of the properties that people can live in that are about the same amount of money as those for rent in that neighborhood.

Your voicemail message can offer to send a copy of these homes to people and ask them to give it to their friends who are getting married. Then in your Evidence of Success you talk about how you are helping somebody who's getting married buy their first home.

In your Letter from the Heart you talk about someone who got married for the first time and how you went to their wedding. Then in your newsletter talk about bridal tips and questions people have when they're buying their first home.

Can you see the congruency between your voicemail message, your Letter from Your Heart, your Evidence of Success, and your Newsletter? Keep a theme that runs every month.

6. Mention there are three things you need to be referred.

People must notice you, think of you, and introduce you.

7. Be real specific about the time you want to call people back.

If you can't be precise, this is the best way to do it:

"I'll be back in the office at 1:00 PM and I'll do my best to get back to you at that time."

8. Every time you listen to your message, record a new one.

This requires a tremendous amount of discipline.

A guy named Chet Holmes wrote a great book called *The Ultimate Selling Machine* in which he says: "The absolute key to success is pig-headed discipline."

It takes pig-headed discipline to change your message and follow these 10 rules.

Always let people know the title you want to be known as, tell them you're working, tell them specifically what you're doing, use future pacing, ask them to imagine calling you, and be specific and congruent in what you're asking for this month.

Remember that people have to notice, think of, and then introduce you. And then offer something that is of great value. The value you offer could be an invitation to a seminar, a free report, a pinpoint analysis of their home, your newsletter, or more.

Be specific about when you're going to call back, or say, *"I'll do my best."*

And remember when you change your message frequently, you've got to keep that pig-headed discipline. If you're going to do it once, you've got to continue to do it all the time.

***Exact Ways to Ask 2* – K Hearts**
To see the video training in the
Magic Words Dojo for this dialogue, go to:
www.byreferralonly.com/WayToAsk2
(you will need to be logged in)

Exact Way to Ask 3

How to Get Your Number into Their Cell Phone Directory!

When you're able to get someone to put your number in their cell phone, your chances of getting introduced go way up!

Listen carefully to the wording in this dialogue.

"When would now be a good time to put my name and phone number in your cell phone directory because the next time you're in a conversation with a person who mentions they will be buying, selling or borrowing you can easily take out your cell phone and look up my number and call me immediately, which means they can get the help they need right away."

You may have noticed the word "now."

People sometimes think that this is a mistake. The truth is it's the perfect embedded command, because it goes directly into the unconscious mind and addresses everything that you want right now. You want that to be done right now.

"When would now be a good time to do this?"

The unconscious mind hears it, but the conscious mind doesn't. They heard the word "now" without noticing and you're giving a directive behind that.

The likelihood of you being introduced to the people that they care about is exponentially greater when your name is in their directory than when it isn't.

It's just undeniable.

Look at your own experiences with the people that you stay in touch with most frequently—friends, family members, past clients, acquaintances. It's usually the people who are in your cell phone directory that you have instant access to and that you are periodically if not regularly calling and staying in touch with.

You don't look up numbers anymore to call people if they're not in your cell phone directory. So the intention is get into their directory as soon as possible.

The 3 Elements You MUST HAVE to Get a Referral

Three things are absolutely necessary to make sure you have consistent, predictable, reliable referrals.

1. People must notice other people.

They've got to know and be aware of when people are in motion. *Motion* means there is something cycling into their life right now that says they're ready to make a move. There's a baby being born, a transfer occurring, a divorce, kids going off to college, or somebody wanting to put an addition on their home.

There are certain things that trigger in people's minds that they may need a real estate consultant or mortgage consultant. It means they're in motion and what you're doing is you're helping people notice others who are in motion.

"The next time you're in a conversation with a person whose kids are going off to college and their house is getting smaller and they're going to downsize…and the next time you're in a conversation with a person who is pregnant and you know they're renting and they're going to need a house soon…and the next time you're in a conversation with a person whose family is expanding with other people moving into their home and they're going to need more space…"

You follow me on this?

What you're doing is helping people notice when people are in motion. People cannot introduce you, refer you, or recommend you until they start to notice people who will need your help.

2. People have to think about you when they notice people.

If they notice, but don't think about you, it doesn't really make a difference that they noticed!

So what you're constantly communicating in all of your dialogues, all of your Letters from the Heart, all of your Evidence of Success, and your newsletters is...

"Who are you noticing right now? Who is in motion right now? Is there anybody right now that's moving here from out of state?"

"Notice right now if you know anyone that recently got a promotion that's probably going to be relocating."

"Notice right now if anybody's mentioned to you that their mortgage is going to be reset and they're not sure what they're going to do next."

3. People have to introduce you.

Introducing means it's an orchestrated introduction, which is the most important part of all, because it doesn't matter if they notice and think of you, if they don't introduce you.

Jerry Spence talks about this in his book *How to Argue and Win Every Time.* He says that you must give explicit instructions to a person on how to perform or how to behave.

What happens if there's somebody lying on the sidewalk and they perhaps fainted and you walk up to them and there's people gathered around and you say: *"Somebody call an ambulance!" "Somebody get some water!" "Somebody get a blanket."*

No one knows who *somebody* is!

The result? No one does anything.

But what would happen if you said this instead...

"In the blue sweater with the red hat on, you go get a blanket. You with the orange skirt, you call 911 right now."

When you give very specific instructions, people move into action immediately.

So when you say...

"The next time you're in conversation with a person who mentions they're going to be moving into a larger, more spacious home because their family is expanding and they need more space, take out your cell phone and look up my number and call me immediately."

That's the instruction on how to behave in that moment and the likelihood of you getting introductions is going to be significantly greater if you follow that formula than if you left it to chance.

DON'T say this:

"Next time you notice somebody who is thinking about making a move, make sure you introduce me to him."

Why? Because there's no immediate action step.

This is a very powerful script that gives you an opportunity to use the dialogue in many different ways.

Here's how you can use this in your emails as a standardized PS:

P.S. The next time you're in a conversation with a person who mentions they'd love to buy a home by the sea, simply take out your cell phone, look up my number and call me immediately, because there's a beautiful home four blocks from the beach with a beautiful 180-degree view currently for sale right now!

The more specific you are in what you're asking for, the more likely people will register the request and respond.

Exact Ways to Ask 3 **– 5 Spades**
To see the video training in the
Magic Words Dojo for this dialogue, go to:
www.byreferralonly.com/WayToAsk3
(you will need to be logged in)

Exact Way to Ask 4

How to Turn a Bad Experience into an Introduction

When somebody says to you something like this...

"I don't know if I want to introduce anyone to you."

"I've done that before and it didn't work well for me."

"If my friends are interested then, they'll call me."

"I just had a bad experience in the past referring people."

It means there's a back story. Here's what you can say to turn those statements around:

"Well, I understand. A great client of mine, Larry, told me that he didn't like giving referrals because he had a bad experience too, and I'm curious, are you comfortable telling me what happened?"

The secret is to really be listening. Then after using good listening skills, continue:

"I'm not going to tell you that it will be different with me, but I will tell you how I will conduct myself with your friends, and then you can tell me how comfortable you are with my approach. Does that seem fair enough?"

Then share your approach and discuss whatever your approach will be:

"I'm going to call and ask them some questions. I'm going to listen to his answers and if I don't think I'm the right consultant to serve him, I will let him know right away. But before I do that, I'm going to show him how I work, and if he doesn't think he's the right client for my consulting services, I'm going to ask him to let me know right away. In that way I

will always start out with whether I think I can help him and whether he thinks I can help, and if not, I'll tell him I can't. I'll give him permission to say that I'm not the right person."

Whenever you're discussing your process, always discuss how you give people permission to reject you.

A lot is going on in this dialogue. It's a very specific script that I want you to memorize to respond when somebody says, *"I've had a bad experience."*

The most important part of all of this is to **listen to the story**. In order for a person to move past a bad experience, they have to fully express the experience and be completely heard.

You want to listen to the story without judging it. Don't say: *"Oh, it's going to be different with me"* or *"No, I won't do it that way"* while they're talking. Be completely engaged in the story because it's their drama.

When somebody has had a bad experience, the thing you want to practice more than anything is listening to their story. Not getting pulled into it, not becoming an advisor around their story, not negating their experience and not saying things like:

"Oh he shouldn't have done that." "Well, you could have done it this way." "No? Really? He did that?"

People just need to discharge a bad experience without any judgment or analysis, and that's what a good listener does. If you pull yourself into the story and start to give advice about what could have happened, I promise you that people will shut down because they don't feel heard in the unconscious part of their mind.

When you look at this dialogue it says, *"I understand. A great client of mine, Larry..."* then you tell the story.

Go on a hunt for a story of somebody who had a bad experience. Tell the story and then mention that when you used your approach they experienced something wonderful because they now feel comfortable referring their friends to you.

Here's what you say to start your story:

"I understand. A great friend of mine, Larry, told me that he didn't like giving referrals because he had a bad experience, too."

It gives people permission to tell their story if someone else has had a similar story.

So when somebody says, *"I've had a really bad experience,"* here's what you say:

"*I understand. I have a great client of mine. His name Is Larry. He had a bad experience, too. I'm curious, are you* ***comfortable*** *telling me about your bad experience?"*

This gives people permission to join the group.

As Dr. Cialdini says, any time you give social proof people will gather around the social proof. So if others had a bad experience, it's okay for me to have one. If no one else has had it, I don't even want to tell my story.

Notice the way I worded this: *"I'm curious, are you* ***comfortable*** *telling me about the experience?"*

Not: *"Will you tell me about it?"*

I'm asking about the level of comfort. It's a great question. It's like when you're driving down the street and you need directions and you stop somebody and say, *"Hey, could you give me directions?"*

"Where are you going?"

"Oh, could you tell me how to get to Starbucks?" Then they give you the directions.

You didn't say, *"Where is Starbucks?"* You said, *"Could you tell me?"*

On the surface the answer is *yes* to that question—yes, they could tell you—but what they say is:

"Yeah, you go down there and take a right, and then you take a left."

What they're answering is the intention of the question not the actual question.

So when you say *"Are you comfortable telling me what happened?"* as opposed to *"Tell me what happened,"* you're addressing them at the unconscious level. If they're comfortable, they'll start telling you their story.

Here's what you say next:

*"Now, I'm **not** going to tell you it will be different with me."*

This is called a negation and the unspoken embedded command underneath it is "***It will be different with me.***" But I'm not going to **tell** you it will be different with me.

You can't say to people *"It will be different with me,"* because their mind will say "Prove it!"

Instead when you put a negative in it, the unconscious mind hears the command ***"It will be different with me."*** The suggestion goes right past the conscious mind and what's sitting in the unconscious mind is *"It will be different with Joe."*

So you can say things like…

*"I'm not going to say **sign the contract** until you're completely comfortable doing so."*

*"I'm not going to say **trust me** until you've looked at all the facts and can see for yourself that you're making a good choice."*

*"I'm not going to say **stop now and work with me** because you'll discover that my role as the person who oversees the transactional details is one of the most important roles in your life."*

So when somebody says, *"I'm just shopping around for rates," you can say:*

*"Well, I'm not going to tell you to **stop doing that** because rates are important. But it only represents a small portion of what a loan consultant does for you."*

You want to pause, raise your voice, downswing, and pause on the phrase "stop doing that," because that's the embedded command.

Negation tells them what to do by showing them you're not going to do that.

It's very powerful because the unconscious mind just hears "Stop doing that" even though you didn't say that. You're not going to say *don't*. You're not going to say *stop doing that because it's a bad idea.*

Whenever we use the word *because,* everything after *because* is three times stronger than what you said before it. *Because* triples the power of everything after it because the mind needs to have a strong, logical reason to justify something.

So whenever you hear me say *because*, it's strengthening everything after that. You don't want to have to explain why you're telling them to "stop doing that" because they will just challenge everything you say.

What Is Your "Approach" When Reaching Out to Their Referral?

What is your approach with people who are introduced to you?

At By Referral Only, our approach when you refer someone to us is:

When you feel comfortable introducing people to By Referral Only, you call our toll-free number and you set up a business development consultation for your friend, and your friend comes onto a call and we spend about an hour on the phone explaining how By Referral Only can help them get from where they are to where they want to go, and you'll feel great that you introduced them to us.

We do TeleClass seminars where you could have your friend come on to a TeleClass seminar and they could listen to us lay out the **before**, **during** and **after** series, and they'll listen and they'll be so happy that you referred them to that class.

They'll actually call you when it's over and say, *"Thank you for doing that"* and you'll feel so good about it.

So what I'm suggesting is there are different ways to introduce people to By Referral Only.

You want to have many different ways that people can introduce people to you, so that you can say to somebody: *"Here is my approach to introduce the people that you care about most to me..."*

"You can either have them call me directly."

"They can go to my blog."

"I have a first-time home buyer seminar."

"I have a website they can go to."

"I have a series of reports that I could send you that you could give to them."

The more ways that people can introduce the people they care about to you, the easier it is for them to do so.

Remember there are three things that have to happen: 1) People have to notice people 2) They have to think of you and 3) They have to introduce you.

The easiest way for people to introduce you is by giving something to a person that the person doesn't already have. The thing you give begins to introduce you.

If they have a friend who is buying their first home, say:

"The easiest way to introduce them to me would be to call me for a free report on 10 questions to ask any real estate agent when you're buying your first home. Call me for that, and then you can give it to your friend and that's the way you introduce your friend to me, by giving your friend something of value that came from me."

That's what we do at By Referral Only. We give a business development consultation, we give a half day seminar, and we give a live teleconference call.

Have something of value you can give to somebody and tell them that's a nice way to introduce you.

***Exact Ways to Ask 4* – 8 Diamonds**
To see the video training in the
Magic Words Dojo for this dialogue, go to:
www.byreferralonly.com/WayToAsk4
(you will need to be logged in)

Exact Way to Ask 5

How to Turn "What Do You Do?" into an Instant Gold Rush of Quality Leads

I imagine that you've frequently been asked, *"What do you do?"*

And I imagine you will be asked the same question many more times in your life. Wouldn't you agree?

It's a question asked in all types of social settings, and it can evoke a response that you either feel confident about or feel some shame about.

There's a quiet conversation going on in the real estate and mortgage business that makes you not want to admit that you do loans or sell homes! So having some strategy to answer that question is going to be helpful.

Here's what to say when someone asks you what you do:

"Well, thanks for asking. The best way to describe it is with a quick story. There was a family that bought a home five years ago and they got involved in an adjustable rate mortgage. It adjusted upward and they found themselves in a position where they weren't capable of making the monthly payment. On top of that, they discovered they owed more on the home than what it's worth.

They were looking at what their options were. Were they going to go to foreclosure, or could they actually sell their home for less than what it was worth and have the bank pick up the difference? They got some advice and the advice they got was predicated on what their dream was. Their dream was to own a home again in the next couple of years. As a result of the advice they got, they are on a path to owning another home and getting a fresh start.

That's what I do. I make dreams come true for people who owe more on their home than it's worth who are planning on buying a home in the next two to three years. I'm a real estate consultant."

You'll notice that when I tell the story I don't introduce myself into the story until the very end.

When I'm answering the question *"What do you do?"* I'm just telling a story about someone else.

The key is whenever you're telling a story to make sure you're telling the story to the person in a way they can relate to it.

If I'm talking to somebody who owns a home and I think they might be upside down right now, the perfect story for them would be a story about someone I helped who was upside down in their mortgage.

If I were talking to a senior right now, they might be downsizing. That would be my story. If I were talking to a young couple in an apartment, I might talk about somebody moving into their first home.

What you tell them that you do for a living has to relate to who you're talking to, versus a generic story that was easy to remember.

You need to be sharp when someone you don't know asks you, *"What do you do?"*

"Well, do you own a home?" If they say yes, you say:

"What I do is make dreams come true. I'm real estate consultant."

"Oh really?"

"Yes. I'm curious…if your best friend lived in an apartment and they wanted to buy a home…" or *"…if your best friend was in a situation where they owed more on their*

home than it was worth," or *"…if your best friend was a senior and they were making a downward move into a smaller, more stress-free environment…*

"…do you have a real estate or mortgage consultant that you would feel comfortable introducing them to?"

This dialogue asks them if they have a real estate consultant, but in an indirect way. If I came out and said "*Do you have a real estate agent?"* that would be a question for the old brain. The old brain is fight and flight. It's the reptilian brain.

If I approach someone and ask *"Do you have a real estate agent?"* they're going to say *"Yes, I'm all handled."*

But if I say…

"If your best friend was going to buy their first home, do you have a real estate consultant you'd feel comfortable introducing them to?"

It causes them to really think. *"Do I have anyone?"* If they say "No" it means they don't have anyone.

Does that make sense?

Here's what you say when they're done answering:

"I'm curious. What would have to happen for you to feel comfortable introducing me to someone that you really care about?"

That's a great question. It's a process question.

The answer might be, *"Well, I'd have to get to know you a little bit better. We need to talk a little bit about it."*

Imagine you're at a cocktail party and someone says, *"Hey, what do you do?"*

"Gosh, that's a great question. Thanks for asking. The best way to describe it is with a quick story. There's a young couple that lived in an apartment. A number of years ago, they were out looking for homes and they were just completely priced out of the market. They noticed that homes were dropping in price significantly. As a matter of fact in the neighborhood they live, they're dropping down 20%, 25%.

They wanted to get some advice if this was the time to move out of their apartment into a home of their own. They got that advice and as a result, they now own a three-bedroom home that was selling for $425,000.00 about a year ago, but was now sold for at $316,000.00 and their house payment is lower than what they're paying for rent.

That's what I do. I make dreams come true for people who were looking for a home two or three years ago who want to buy today and get their house payments equivalent to what they pay in rent."

They say, *"Oh really?"*

"Yes. I'm curious. If your best friend was going to move out of an apartment into a home of their own, do you have a real estate or mortgage consultant that you'd feel real comfortable introducing them to?"

They say, *"No."*

"Oh you don't? Well, I'm wondering what would have to happen for you to feel comfortable introducing me to the people that you care about."

When people say *"What do you do?"* you want three things to happen:

First, you want them to be more interested in what you're going to say after you're done saying it. So when you tell them your story, you want them to be more interested in who you are than before they knew what you did.

We have a tendency when somebody says, *"What do you do?"* to say, *"Oh, I'm in real estate,"* and people then become less interested in you. It's like going into a party yelling, *"Fire. I'm a realtor."*

Second, you want people to feel so comfortable that they decide to give you their email address or their phone number, and they look forward to staying in contact with you.

Third, quickly discover if they are the type of person you do not want to work with. If they say in a condescending tone, "*Oh you're in real estate?"* you say, *"Yes, but I'm thinking about getting out. Hand me the ketchup, will you?"*

If that's the way they're going to react to you, you're not going to try to persuade them that you're the person to help them.

***Exact Ways to Ask 5* – Q Diamonds**
To see the video training in the
Magic Words Dojo for this dialogue, go to:
www.byreferralonly.com/WayToAsk5
(you will need to be logged in)

Exact Way to Ask 6

The Answer to "How's Business?" that Results in a Closed Transaction 20% of the Time!

Here's what the answer to "How's Business?" should sound like:

"Things are going well and isn't it nice to know that I have time for you, your family, your friends or anyone else you know and like who could use my help right now? I'm curious, who do you know who would love to own their own home, because when you introduce them to me they can better understand what their best options are in today's marketplace."

I love this script. This is one of the first dialogues I started to work with that got things into casual conversation and you'll come across frequently when people say, *"How's business"* or *"How's the market?"*

A good thought to remember is to be neutral in your voice tone. Move away from *"Oh, it's great!!!!"* which sounds like I don't need you or *"Unbelievable"* which is ambiguous.

What you're attempting to do is move the conversation. So when somebody asks you how business is, ask yourself...

"Do I choose to have a conversation now?" Or, *"Do I choose to disengage because I could use this as an opening or as a close?"*

"How's business?"

"Oh, fabulous. We are doing great right now."

End of conversation.

"How is business?"

"Well, it's going well and isn't it nice to know that I have time for you and your family and your friends and your neighbors and anyone else you know and like who could use my help right now? I'm curious…who do you know who would love to own their own home? Or maybe you know someone who would love to take advantage of this marketplace and maybe purchase a foreclosure for their first investment property and you could introduce them to me so they can better understand what their best options are right now."

It's a wonderful way to step into asking for a referral. When somebody asks you how business is they think you are going to talk about business, but you end up talking about who they could introduce you to.

Close your eyes for a minute and just ask yourself: When's the last time somebody asked you how business was, and then think about how you responded.

You know it's going to happen again. You know that you're going to move into your future and there's somebody in the near future who's going to come up to you and say, "How's business?"

So now you have this new choice. You could use that as just a rhetorical question. A question people ask that they really don't want an answer to and they're not really interested in your answer. They just don't even know what else to ask.

So you're at a party and they say, *"Hey, how's business?"*

"Oh, it's going well. Isn't it nice to know that you have somebody who has time for you, for your family, your friends?"

"Yes, pass me the ketchup." Well that shows they really weren't even interested. They just didn't know what else to ask.

Now that you have this awareness you can decide…

Is this a moment to move into introduction or are they asking it rhetorically?

Most of your business comes from casual conversation. You know that it happens when you're at a cocktail party and somebody bumps into you and says, *"Hey, how's business?"*

It happens that way, and if you can get conversational with them you say, *"Well, you know what? It's going really well and isn't it nice to know?"*

That's called compliance. When you say: *"Isn't it nice to know,"* it's nearly impossible to disagree with.

"Isn't it nice to know that I do have time for you ***and*** *your family* ***and*** *your friends* ***and*** *anyone else you know* ***and*** *like who could* ***use my help*** *right now?"*

Every time you see a comma in a script, you could use the word "and" instead to get people into trance when you say: ***"Isn't it nice to know*** *that I have time for you* ***and*** *your family* ***and*** *your friends* ***and*** *anyone else you know and like?"*

Keep going *"and, and, and, and"* and people will keep dropping down lower after every "and" into a trance and now you're talking to the unconscious mind.

"Who could use my help right now? Who would like to buy their first home right now and I'm curious who you know who would love to take advantage of this marketplace?"

I love the word "love." Love has such a high frequency to it. *"Who do you know who would* ***love*** *to get their home sold right now?"*

"Who do you know who would ***love*** *to move out of an apartment into a home of their own?"*

"Who do you know who would **love** *to refinance right now because they have a mortgage that's about to reset and they're scared?"*

If you embed the word "love" and make it a really important concept it helps people look further for you as opposed to saying just, *"Who do you know who wants to buy or sell a house?"*

Remember this: Everything after the word "because" becomes three times stronger because the mind loves reasons for things.

So when you say, *"I'm curious who do you know who would love to own their own home because…"* Everything that comes next is strong because you're giving a reason.

"…because when you introduce them to me, they can better understand what their best options are in today's marketplace."

***Exact Ways to Ask 6* – 3 Spades**
To see the video training in the
Magic Words Dojo for this dialogue, go to:
www.byreferralonly.com/WayToAsk6
(you will need to be logged in)

<u>Exact Way to Ask 7</u>

Answer "How's the Market?" through Your Client's Eyes

Now let's look at the right way to answer the question "How's the market?"...

"Experience shows it all depends on where you live. I would love to do some research for you and send you an email that will tell you what homes are for sale, what homes have sold recently and how long those homes are taking to sell in your neighborhood. This way you can feel secure in the knowledge that you have the most accurate information that will tell you right away how the market is right now. I imagine that information would be valuable to you, would it not?"

Underline the embedded commands in that statement. The embedded commands are one to four words that could stand on their own, and when you speak them they go directly into the unconscious mind.

When you embed a command, you pause right before you embed the command. You raise your voice slightly, insert the command, and then pause again.

The first embedded command in the answer above is ***you can feel secure***.

The second embedded command is ***that information would be valuable to you***. There are more than four words here, but they're silent words so "information valuable to you" is the command.

The dialogue would sound like this:

"Hey Joe, how's the market?"

*"Well that's a great question. Experience shows that it depends on where you live. I would love to do some research for you and send you an email that will tell you what homes are for sale now, what homes have sold recently and how long those homes are taking to sell in your neighborhood so... **you can feel secure**."*

When I get to the end of the embedded command, I pause before continuing.

*"...you can feel secure... in the knowledge that you have the most accurate information. Now this timely information will tell you right away how your market is right now **and**..."*

Whenever there's a comma or a period, you can use the word "and" instead to create trance. *"And, and, and, and."* The more "ands" you use in your sentence the deeper people drop into the story.

*"**And** then this is what happened. **And** then this is what happened. **And** then this is what happened. **And** then you should have seen what happened next **and** then..."*

What you're saying becomes one long story as it's spoken. Spoken language is often very different than written language, so when I make those adjustments, notice that.

How to Answer Every Question through Your Client's Eyes

Standing in line one day at Starbuck's, there was a young lady right in front of me, and I just got this notion.

I said to her, *"So what do you do for a living?"*

She turns to me and she says, "I'm a real estate agent."

I said, *"How's the market?"*

And she gave me what a typical agent or lender would say. She said, "It's picking up."

Picking up…that's an interesting concept because she's talking about ***her*** market when I was asking about ***my*** market.

People have a tendency to answer questions through their own eyes instead of through the eyes of the person who asked the question. **But there is another way.**

It's called *see-through vision*.

The idea is to answer every question through your client's eyes instead of your own. So when somebody says, *"How is* ***the*** *market,"* what they're really saying is, *"How is* ***my*** *market?"*

See the difference?

And what I've learned as I've traveled all over the country is that there is no one market.

The market in Virginia is very different than Laguna Beach, very different than in L.A., very different than Chula Vista, very different than Escondido. It's very, very different depending on where you are.

A coastal area is very different than the other side of the freeway so when somebody asks you about the market you say, *"Well experience shows it depends on where you live."*

This is called a *reframing statement*.

By reframing it, you remove it from being too general.

Then you use another technique called *chunking down* —chunking specifically into the person's market rather than your own.

So the agent in line at Starbucks didn't say, *"Well it depends on where you live."* She said, *"It's picking up,"* and she was chunking in the direction of her market.

She chuckled when I told her what I did. I said, *"Are you open for a little coaching? Because when I asked you how the market was what I was really referring to is I live right up the street on Cambridge Street and I'm wondering about four or five homes that are for sale in our area right now. What are they for sale for? How long are they taking to sell? How is it affecting the impact of the homes in my neighborhood? That's what I'm really curious about, my self-interest."*

So even when you're on the phone in your hour of power you could say to a person:

"Hey, one of the most common questions I get is 'How is the market?' and here is what my answer is when they ask: It all depends where your friend lives, and if you have a friend or a family member who would like to get some research on what homes are selling for in their neighborhood I'd love to provide that for them."

Are you following me on this? You can preempt that question; you can predict that the question is going to be asked.

If you are at a party chatting with someone, you can just say…

"You know, one of the questions I'm frequently asked is, 'How's the market?' and I just want to share with you guys how I'm answering that right now because in my experience it shows that it really depends on where people live and I would love to do research for all of you…

…and this is what I do for my friends and family members and the people I care about is I put an email together and I send it out to them every month and it shows them what homes are for sale, what homes have sold and

how long they're taking to sell. That way you can feel secure in the knowledge that you have."

You can use this dialogue as a way to drive conversation to add people to your database. It's a simple way to access somebody's name, address and phone number to put them into some type of an auto-responder that sends them some type of monthly update.

You might even consider walking around with a little name badge that says, **"Ask me how the market is."** As soon as people find that you're in the real estate or the mortgage business, it's their unconscious question so you might as well start addressing it before it's even asked.

Every time you're with somebody you know they want to know how the market is. They want to know how *their* market is, so address it from their perspective.

***Exact Ways to Ask 7* – A Spades**
To see the video training in the
Magic Words Dojo for this dialogue, go to:
www.byreferralonly.com/WayToAsk7
(you will need to be logged in)

Exact Way to Ask 8

Get 5 Times More Introductions When You Start with the End in Mind!

"Isn't it nice to know" is a very simple phrase to create compliance.

Compliance is one of the more important concepts in influence, because in order for a person to say *yes* at the end of a process they have to say *yes* many times to small agreements.

So when you ask them at the end to *"Sign this,"* it's not the first time they're saying *yes*. Here's how you can gain compliance:

*"**Isn't it nice to know** that the phone number you just called me on is the same number you can give your friends when they need real estate or mortgage help?"*

*"**Isn't it nice to know** that I would give your friends the help they need to reach their goals? By the way, who is the next person you know that is most likely to do what you just did?"*

By the time you ask the important question, they may have said yes a hundred times consciously and unconsciously to direct questions and rhetorical questions in your conversation.

*"**Isn't it nice to know** that you have a friend in the business who you can feel real comfortable telling the people you care about most to?"*

That's a rhetorical question. You're not really asking them to answer you. The unconscious mind will answer it, *"**Yes** it's nice."* You're really making a suggestion, not asking a question.

Here's another example:

*"**Isn't it nice to know** that the phone number you just called me on is the same one you could give to your friends?"*

I could have said, *"You could give that same phone number that you called on to your friends,"* but I would be making a statement without compliance ahead of it. I want to get momentum into the command. So I start with, "Isn't it nice?"

*"**Isn't it nice to know** that when we're all done today you'll feel comfortable signing a listing agreement? And if you're not comfortable signing a listing agreement, we can still talk about it before you sign the listing agreement."*

I've embedded the words *sign the listing agreement* three times. You're discovering now that by using Magic Words this ambiguity allows their unconscious mind to arrive at its own conclusions as opposed to you telling them the conclusions.

When you say, *"We're going to sign a listing contract today,"* the conscious mind resists.

But when you say:

*"You may or may not **sign a listing contract today** and I would never ask you to **sign a listing agreement** unless all of your questions were answered first and isn't it nice to know that you're working with somebody who isn't going to **ask you to sign** anything until you're **really comfortable**?"*

There are a lot of embedded commands here, with a lot of compliance occurring. I want you to learn how to speak a little more ambiguously like this, but also know what your intention is when you speak.

Here's Why Every Good Communication Starts with a Well-Formed Outcome!

The question you need to ask is:

What outcome do I want when I'm done with this conversation?

For instance, if you were watching me on video now, you might hear me say…

"Isn't it nice to know that you're watching this on video? Isn't it nice to know that you're actually at home right now or in your office at whatever time of the day that it is right now where you and you can play this over and over again? Isn't that a nice thing to know that you can do that? Isn't it nice to know that you could download the notes and look at them any time you want? And isn't it nice to know that you could listen to the audio over and over again?"

As I say those commands, I'm building "*yes, yes, yes, yes, yes, yes"* in the listener's mind.

The next time you're meeting a client, think how you can create compliance before you start your consultation.

To build compliance at a live event, you might hear me say, *"Hey, welcome to Chicago. It's Monday. You're in your chair. You're listening to me. You're comfortable."*

So my audience members are saying **yes** it is Monday. **Yes** I am in my chair. **Yes** I am listening to him. And then when I say, *"and you're comfortable,"* the command ***you're comfortable*** gets in.

"Yes, yes, yes, comfortable."

I do this instead of saying, *"You're comfortable to be here,"* which causes the unconscious mind to think, *"I haven't agreed to that."*

It takes at least three commands in order for something to become a pattern.

So, when I say, *"It's Monday morning. You're in your seats. You're listening to me. And you're comfortable."* That's four: "yes, yes, yes, yes."

Now when you walk into a client's house you would say, *"Gosh, it's Monday. You're here. I'm here, and I wouldn't ask you to **sign** anything until you're **really comfortable**."*

You've used the embedded command ***sign*** because that's what you're there for them to do. And you've built compliance. *"**Yes**, it's Monday. **Yes**, I'm here. **Yes**, you're here. **Yes**, you won't ask me to sign anything until I'm comfortable."*

If you can make a command of what you want the outcome to be in one or two words, and then state it in the first 30 seconds after compliance, you get them moving in the direction of where you want the outcome to go.

The secret is to always know exactly what you want the outcome to be at the end of your communication and be able to state it in two to three words.

Embed your goal over and over again, along with compliance ahead of it.

One of the statements that creates compliance is, *"Isn't it nice to know?"*

Whenever you're about to say something ask yourself if you can put this phrase in front of it so you get a little mini agreement before you make your bigger suggestion.

Isn't it nice to know that your unconscious has the answers to all the questions you'll ever ask?

Isn't it nice to know you have all the resources you need right now within you?

Isn't it nice to know you can integrate this learning at the speed that best serves you?

Isn't that nice to know?

***Exact Ways to Ask 8* – K Diamonds**
To see the video training in the
Magic Words Dojo for this dialogue, go to:
www.byreferralonly.com/WayToAsk8
(you will need to be logged in)

Exact Way to Ask 9

Help People Recognize Your Value

Why is it so important to get others to recognize your value?

Because once they recognize it, you can ask them to refer you to others who want the same value!

Value is received only when it's recognized.

That means it's your responsibility to help people recognize your value.

When a client says, *"Thank you,"* you have a moment to help them recognize that value by saying:

"My pleasure. You'd do the same for me."

This is one of the most powerful statements you can ever make. Why?

Because when somebody performs a favor, the person getting the favor feels better about it than the person giving it.

There's a catch though...

As time goes on, this "rule" reverses. After a while the person who received the favor remembers and values it less and the person who gave the favor remembers and values it more.

As soon as you do a favor for someone they usually say, *"Oh, thank you."*

Most of the time you say, *"No problem."*

Then two weeks later the person who got the favor is saying vaguely, *"Oh, yeah, I remember you helped me cut the grass."* But now you're thinking...

"Don't you remember how I had to go and get the lawnmower from my brother's house and..."

The more time goes by, the less they remember and value the favor. At the same time, the more *you* value the favor you did.

Does that make sense?

That's why it's so critical that the moment a person recognizes your value you say, *"Hey, thank you so much, that's great and I know under the same circumstances, I could count on you to do the very same thing for me."*

You freeze frame the moment and then, as if you're thinking it over, you say, *"...Yeah, I know you'd do the same for me."*

Here's another wonderful way to help people recognize your value:

"Can I ask you to share with me what you believe was the most valuable thing that I've done for you? I just want to hear what you have to say because I believe I know what I did, but I'm curious, what do you think the most valuable thing I did for you was?"

Listen really carefully to how they answer because they're using their ***hot words.***

"Oh, thank you so much. I really appreciate everything you're doing for me."

You would say, *"Well, I appreciate you saying that and I know that I could always count on you under similar situations, too. I'm curious could you tell me what you value most about what I've done for you?"*

Whatever words they say next, those are ***hot***. Suppose they say, *"You've been so patient and so thorough with all of the details on the transaction. We're so grateful."*

Their hot words are: ***patient, thorough, grateful*** and those are the words you use over and over again in your future communications.

When you hang up the phone, immediately you write a note:

"Bob, great talking to you. When you express that you trust in my patience and feel grateful for my thoroughness, remember those are the same things that I will do when you recommend a friend or a family member to me. As a matter of fact, they'll say to you, 'Joe is so patient. He's so thorough. We're so grateful.' Enclosed are a couple of my business cards."

You're using their own words to influence them.

A friend of mine, Eben Pagan says, *"Value isn't what you say it is. Value is what your customer says it is."*

Did You Know There Are the Different Levels of Value?

Money has value, people have value, ideas have value, but the most valuable thing that people can say about you is about your character or your energy.

At the lowest value, everyone can cut a commission and save people money.

At the next level, everyone can introduce someone to a good resource—a title company, carpet cleaner, etc.—that has value.

The next level of value is your ideas, strategies and methods. When you talk about selling their home, one of the most valuable things you could show a person is the *"37 Ways to Sell Your Own Listing"* that you can find in the Getting Listings program, and download that booklet.

So when somebody says, *"What are you going to do to get my home sold?"* you could say to them...

"Well, I focus on the strategies and ideas that help me get your listing sold, and I have 37 things that I concentrate on to sell your listing."

These strategies go beyond the value of *the people you know* and *cutting the commission*, because they are unique to you.

The more unique it is to you, the more the value is perceived.

Now let's talk about the absolute highest level of value...

It's spiritual or energetic value. It's when people trust and feel comfortable with you.

"I don't really know what it is about you Joe, but I just trust that you've got my best interests at heart."

That's the kind of thing we find the most valuable.

I could cut my commission, I could introduce you to people, I could have strategies that sell your house, but the most valuable thing is in my energy, spirit, or character.

Does that make sense to you?

When you ask people, *"Hey, so tell me what you think the most valuable thing is that I've done for you?"* listen carefully.

Are they valuing you at the monetary level, the resource level, the strategy level, or the character level?

You'll notice that most people will start to feel more compelled to introduce you when they start to value your character. They start to value who you are more than what you do.

"What you really did was that you saved us a lot of money."

This level of value is not nearly as great as:

"Well, Joe, you're so thorough. We're really grateful. You really gave us advice that we could trust. You were patient with us every step of the way."

Can you see that?

You know you have somebody who will go out of their way to make sure that they introduce you to the people they care about when they say, *"Hey, my friend called and told me that you really did a great job. You were patient. You were really thorough and he's really trusted you, too."*

Notice how different this is from...

"My friend said you'll cut your commission like you do for everyone else."

The most important point here is around the whole notion of reciprocity.

Reciprocity is at its high point the moment you deliver value and it begins to diminish very quickly. That is one reason why you want to have real meaningful, deep referral conversations when people recognize your value.

So when somebody says, *"Wow! Thank you,"* you've got to look at that as the high point of reciprocity.

You've got to think, *"With every tick of the clock, they'll see my value less than they do right at this moment,"* and so now is the time to step in and say:

"Is this a good time that we can talk a little bit about the different ways that you see me providing value for you? Because I really would love to hear what you think is of value; I'd love to hear what I've done for you is of value to you."

Then listen for their ***hot words*** and when you get their hot words you can start to ask for introductions.

***Exact Ways to Ask 9* – 10 Hearts**
To see the video training in the
Magic Words Dojo for this dialogue, go to:
www.byreferralonly.com/WayToAsk9
(you will need to be logged in)

Exact Way to Ask 10

How to Use Secret Persuasion Patterns to Make It Easy for People to Introduce You to People They Know

How well do you follow through when someone tells you about a referral?

What's the process for setting an appointment with that referral?

Suppose your client says, *"Hey, my mom's thinking about moving or refinancing."*

In a referral conversation, you would say, *"Brent, would **you be comfortable** telling your mom about me?"*

Brent says, *"Yes, I would."*

*"Well, I know that telling your mom is the easy part. I also know that getting me and your mom into a conversation is the hard part. So I'm curious, what do you think would be the best way to **make sure** that your mom and I get into a conversation very soon?"*

I love this dialogue. This is one of my most powerful dialogues because it's used in the moment when a person says, *"Hey, my sister's thinking about moving."*

*"Oh, that's great. Would **you be comfortable*** (embedded command) *telling your mom about me?"*

"Oh, yes. I would love her to work with you."

"Well, the easy part is just telling me about your mom. Do you know what the hard part is? Getting the two of us into a conversation, because if you were me, what would you do to make sure that we get into a conversation?"

This dialog takes them from suggesting they know someone, to an action called *introduction*.

The referral actually begins when they introduce you to people they know.

How many times in your past has somebody said, *"My mom's thinking about moving,"* and you said, *"Would you give her my card?"* Or, *"Would you tell her about me?"*

And so they did, and nothing happened?

Inner Circle Member Jae Wu and I had the following situation happen to us, and it's a beautiful example of how this dialogue works in real the real world.

I was on the phone with Jae, and I said, *"Hey Jae, there's a guy in my acting comedy class that was telling me about his need to get a loan and to buy a home and I told him all about you."*

Jae instantly said, *"Joe, what did you say about me?"*

"I told him to give you a call and I gave him your phone number!"

Jae said, *"Well, you know, Joe, that's the easy part. The hard part's making sure the two of us get together. What do you think is going to be the best way to make sure that I talk to this guy?"*

"Well, what if I do this? What if I email him right now and I'll cc you, and then you could read it and then if he wants to respond to that email, we'll see what happens."

Then I took the email introduction template right off the By Referral Only website, customized it, and sent it over to him. He came up to me later at class and said, *"Hey, I talked to Jae, thanks!"*

I facilitated the introduction because Jae responded in the moment, *"What's the best way to get us connected? How are you going to get us into a conversation?"*

A few days later I got a thank you card and $5.00 Starbucks card from Jae.

Did You See the Four Secret Persuasion Patterns Hidden Inside This Dialogue?

1. Secret Persuasion Pattern 1

Get compliance first.

When somebody says, *"Hey, my mom's thinking about moving..."*

Before you say, *"Would you introduce her to me,"* get compliance by asking: *"Would **you be comfortable** introducing me to her?"*

You'll get a small *yes*, but more importantly, you'll make the embedded command "be comfortable."

So when you say, *"Would you be comfortable introducing her to me?"* you're embedding "be comfortable" even as you're getting compliance.

2. Secret Persuasion Pattern 2

Create an unconscious challenge.

There's a part of the mind that likes to take on a challenge.

Instead of saying, *"Hey, could you set up a conversation with your mom and I?"* which can cause resistance...

You can challenge them by saying, *"Telling her is the easy part. Having us get into a conversation is the hard part."*

They'll want to rise to your challenge saying, "*No, it's not hard. I can get you into a conversation.*"

3. Secret Persuasion Pattern 3

Embed a command of certainty. The key words are "**make sure**."

"I know that getting me and your mom into a conversation is the hard part. I'm curious, what do you think is the best way to ***make sure*** (embedded command) *we get into a conversation?"*

You're not asking, *"What's the best way to get us into a conversation?"*

You're asking how to "make sure" we get into a conversation.

4. Secret Persuasion Pattern 4

At the moment of referral, orchestrate the introduction immediately. As soon as the person identifies their referral, that's when this dialogue is most applicable. It has to happen automatically.

Among some people who learn this, there is a feeling that, *"This is way too pushy. If people want to introduce me, they will."*

Well, that may be true, but your competitive difference comes from identifying a referral and walking away with a future introduction planned. That's your competitive edge.

Sure, the introduction can wait. But if you let it wait, you don't know what's going to happen and more than likely your potential client will stumble into another agent who has mastered this dialogue and you just lost that client for life.

So it's probably best that you master this dialogue, don't you agree?

***Exact Ways to Ask 10* – 2 Diamonds**
To see the video training in the
Magic Words Dojo for this dialogue, go to:
www.byreferralonly.com/WayToAsk10
(you will need to be logged in)

Exact Way to Ask 11

How to Use a Six-Word Pattern that Quickly Interrupts to Plant a Referral Seed

"Please don't keep me a secret."

This is called a pattern interrupt because the word "don't" is quickly converted mentally to "I don't" and the word "secret" is one of the eleven *implosion* words that cause the mind to say, "What secret?"

The word "don't" in some circles—maybe yours—is the most commonly heard word before the age of four. *"Don't do that. Don't do that. Don't do that."* And if you've raised children, you know that the response is *"I'm not."*

"Don't pull Mary's hair."

"I'm not. She pulled mine first."

In the brain, "don't" causes an instant opposite reaction. *"Don't keep me a secret"* makes us automatically think, *"I'm not going to keep you a secret."*

Here's the key…

This dialog only applies when it's spoken; it's never written. If you write the words, *"Don't keep me a secret,"* what gets remembered is the negation, *"Keep me a secret."*

"Don't keep me a secret" is a pattern interrupt designed to allow you to easily plant a hypnotic referral suggestion with the next thing you say. What you say after the pattern interrupt counts the most, so end your conversations with a powerful suggestion, like this:

"Bob, great talking to you. Please don't keep me a secret."

When they say, *"I won't,"* you say…

"I appreciate you saying that because when you tell your friends and your family members that you really care about them, then they'll get the advice they want."

The words "don't keep me a secret" interrupt the "goodbye" pattern so they can hear what you say next.

You'll find a great place to do this is on the telephone. For example, you're on the phone and the person is about to hang up. They say, *"Okay, I'll talk to you later".*

Here's what you can say next:

"Hey, please don't keep me a secret."

They'll likely say something like, *"Oh, no, I tell everybody about you."*

You must follow through immediately with a powerful suggestion or question:

"Hey, when you tell everybody about me, is there anyone specifically you've talked to that could use my help right now?"

***Exact Ways to Ask 11* – 3 Diamonds**
To see the video training in the
Magic Words Dojo for this dialogue, go to:
www.byreferralonly.com/WayToAsk11
(you will need to be logged in)

<u>Exact Way to Ask 12</u>

Be the Strong Person They're Looking for to Overcome Procrastination

What do you do when you hear something like this?

"My dad is moving and he needs an agent or a lender, but I'm not really comfortable referring or recommending him to you."

If you've ever heard any version of that before, you know there's this awkward of moment silence.

Here are the Magic Words you can use to overcome it...

"Well Larry, I really appreciate that ***and*** *I'm glad that* ***you trust me*** *enough to be honest with me."*

A nice pause...

*"...**and** a few months from now when your dad is calling you* ***and*** *thanking you for introducing me to him, you'll look back at this moment* ***and*** *laugh about how you wer slightly concerned before you decided to* ***introduce me to him and*** *feeling good because he is the person that you really care about* ***and*** *I imagine you want him to get the best advice possible from someone* ***you believe in****, don't you?"*

This is a complex language pattern because you're dealing with hesitancy.

What do people really want when they hesitate?

Leadership.

Emerson said, *"The mass of men are silently begging to be led."*

So when somebody is hesitant, they're looking for someone who is stronger than their urge to delay, procrastinate or hold back.

There's a lot going on in this dialogue because it leads someone's thoughts from where they're at to a new place where you want them to go.

The Power of Future Pacing

A Magic Words technique to show leadership is called *future pacing*.

It's an advanced strategy and very powerful. When you learn how to use it in the months and years ahead, you'll easily be a better leader.

In the future when you're using this technique regularly, you're going to say to yourself, *"This was a magical moment learning this dialogue and learning this technique."*

One of the most important things you'll learn when you're asking for a referral is how to help people experience an advance feeling of how they're going to feel once they give you their referral.

Always remember and never forget the number one reason people refer is for how *they* feel.

Future pacing means suggesting the good feelings people will feel in the future, and getting them to feel that future feeling now.

You let them experience right now what it's going to feel like when they do refer someone to you.

Did You Notice the Trance Language?

Notice the trance word ***and***. You can count the number of "ands" that are inside the dialog.

Every "and" drops a person down a little deeper into a trance.

I'm cautious of using that word *trance* because it has a tone of manipulation. But if you look up the word *manipulate* it means to move with intent—and you can manipulate for good reasons and you can manipulate for bad reasons. The word *trance* only refers to a form of disassociation.

A trance is a natural state we all experience from time to time. Daydreaming is a form of a trance. When we daydream we focus on something internal that causes us to decrease our awareness of what's happening around us right now. That's all a trance is.

You could even be in a trance right now, as you read this.

You could be focused inward, having an internal story going on about what I'm talking about right now and not even be aware of what's going on with your right leg until I just brought it into awareness.

When you use trance language in a dialog, what you're doing is creating a future picture that people are putting themselves into in which they're no longer aware of what's happening in the moment right now.

When you *future pace* using trance language, you help people experience the kind of feeling you want them to have in the future when they refer someone to you.

You want them to have that feeling now.

Here's How You Can Mesmerize Them!

The concept of trance language was introduced by a guy named Frank Mesmer.

Now you know the root of the word "mesmerize."

Frank Mesmer first talked about the natural condition of hypnosis, or the idea that we can get into a hypnotic trance, a state called *mesmerized*.

When you're in a trance, your focus becomes very narrow and your internal imagery is an unfolding story. You can become mesmerized by the story, so immersed that you feel like you're in it. Stories are very trance-like.

So let me tell you a story.

Imagine a seawall and a path along it on one side and the beach on the other...

Several summers ago a teacher was sitting on the seawall, resting and eating a sandwich while observing events on the beach.

There were two young boys about six years old playing together and running around, having a lot of fun. When they got tired from all the activity, they sat down near the teacher and began talking to one another.

The teacher was listening carefully to their language.

Perhaps these kids had just met or maybe they had known each other for a while, but she was just observing and listening, noticing the rate at which the kids talked and which kid talked more and which kid talked less.

Finally the teacher said to the boys, *"What do you want to be when you grow up?"*

"I'm going to be a brain surgeon."

The other kid said, *"Gosh, I don't really know what I'll be. I never thought about what I want to be. I'm not that bright, I know that. I'm not that smart to be a brain surgeon."*

The kids got up and ran off and the teacher sat there wondering where that second little boy's development of his belief had come from.

She thought it probably came from another teacher or a parent or someone else, because at the age of six it didn't come from true experience.

She thought that if he doesn't have anyone to help him change his belief it will affect him the rest of his life. That limiting sense of possibility will hold him back from his potential.

Beliefs are not true. They are constructs around which we organize our behaviors, so we act as if our beliefs are true. We believe that every belief is true. For that reason, our beliefs come true.

Beliefs are either *empowering* or *limiting* or *self-fulfilling* prophecies.

I love when people say to me, *"Trances are manipulation."*

Well, that's their belief and that belief will guide them whenever they hear the word "trance."

Alternatively they can decide:

"Trance language is a way for me to help influence people to move in the direction of the dream that they have, and it's incumbent upon me to help them feel the way they will feel in the future when they do feel comfortable referring someone to me."

I can help them expand their sense of possibility.

Exact Ways to Ask 12 **– 4 Diamonds**
To see the video training in the
Magic Words Dojo for this dialogue, go to:
www.byreferralonly.com/WayToAsk12
(you will need to be logged in)

Exact Way to Ask 13

Master Both Parts of Every Transaction

There are two parts to every transaction: the **product** and the **process**.

What you're really saying is there's a thing called buying a house, the actual house. There's also a thing called getting a loan, the actual money. When you sell your house to get the money...that's the product.

Then there's the other part of it, called the process. That's what you feel like when you're buying a house, when you're selling a house, and when you're borrowing money. It's the feeling you have.

When you put the product and the process together, you create what is called an experience.

We live in a whole new economy today. It's called the experience economy.

The experience economy is different from a goods economy. A goods economy is just the product. It's all about the goods or commodities. Wherever goods are for sale, it's all about the price. So when you're only talking about the product, your conversation is primarily going to be about price.

Notice that if your client is always asking you, *"Can you cut your commission? Will you reduce the fees? Can we do it cheaper? What's the highest price I can get?"* they see what they're doing as a commodity—an exchange of a goods for money—not an experience.

Service is different and moves us in the right direction. When you say, *"I give good service,"* you're moving past the product.

For instance, Nordstrom's gives good service. I wouldn't call it an experience, but I would call it good service. The clothes, the product, the goods you can get anywhere, but when you go to Nordstrom's you get good service along with the product which allows them to charge a higher price.

Now what makes something into an experience?

It's the element of time. The longer you spend with somebody, the more it becomes an experience.

When I go to Disneyland, I'm not looking at the goods or the services. I'm looking at it as an experience, a fun time to spend with my family building memories.

When I go to NIKETOWN, it's an experience. They have the gym shoes—the goods. They have helpful people—the service. But the environment that's fun to hang around in —that's the experience.

When people are going through the process of buying a home, getting a loan, or selling their home, it's a total experience. And guess what? You're in charge of creating that for them.

Can you see how this is a very different economy than a goods or service economy.

Refer to what you do as an experience.

"When you buy a home from me, it's an experience. It's beyond just the home. It's beyond just good service. It's a complete experience."

If you go to O'Hare Airport in Chicago, there is a parking garage where each floor is a different representation of one sports team. When you park in the lot, you park in front of a particular sports player. It could be Michael Jordan's spot or Scottie Pippen's spot or Dick Butkus' spot or Jack Cannon's spot or any of the old-time football or baseball players like Ernie Banks' spot or Ron Santo's spot. When you pull in, you are greeted by their voice—they greet you to that spot. For that pleasure, you pay about 25% more for the experience.

The service is how the person treats you when you're paying. But what you're feeling as you're parking is the experience.

It's when the kids say, *"Mom! Mom! See if you can get Ron Santo's spot." "Mom, I want to park next to Ernie Banks."* That's when you're in the new economy, called the experience economy.

How to Know the Difference between a Service and an Experience

Service is something you deliver. Experience is something you stage.

When you're providing a service, it's intangible. When you're providing an experience, it's memorable.

When you're providing a service, it's customized. When you're providing an experience, it's personal.

Service is delivered on demand. Experience is revealed over time. as people go through the current experience with you, they are in the "during" timeline and things are revealed to them…the popcorn letter comes…then the "ducks in a row" letter…then all the other By referral Only touch points that wow the client.

As opposed to good service, orchestrating an experience is predictable. For example, when your client discovers you pay for their babysitters so they can come into your office, they have a different experience of you even before meeting you in your office for the first time!

When you complete the initial appointment, you give them moving boxes. Experience is unexpected and revealed every step of the way, becoming more exciting with every step because it is a whole different experience to what most people have ever experienced.

*"I have never **experienced** getting a loan or buying a home or selling a home like this before."*

In service, people are clients. In an experience, people are more like guests. They're guests in your life. They're guests in the experience of helping them buy, sell, or borrow.

In service, people see the benefit. In experience, they feel it as a sensation. They associate a feeling to it, more than an acquisition to it.

Services are activities performed for clients. Experience is very personal.

Most home buyers and sellers get distracted by the search for a service or commodity. They go out looking for a real estate agent or a house. They treat real estate agents like a commodity, as opposed to their own unique individual experience creator. They treat the house hunt or sale as a transaction, not as an experience. They look for a transaction facilitator, not an experience creator.

So as you go through this dialogue, you're communicating to people that you're going to create an experience for them of buying, selling, or borrowing. It's something they'll get to experience, not something you'll tell them about.

Remember: **You tell people about service. You reveal experience**.

How to Create Winning Experiences for Your Clients

You want to start talking about the experience by morphing the conversation over to a restaurant they love.

(Stay with me on this I know you'll like it by the time you're done learning it!)

Start your inquiry with this question sequence:

Can you tell me what your favorite local restaurant is?

Is it your favorite because they have both great food and great service?

Imagine that the food is the product and the service is the process.

I'm curious; does your favorite local restaurant do much advertising?

Probably not because their food and their service are outrageously good \and most of their business comes from repeat guests and referrals, does it not?

So for just a moment, can you ***imagine that I am just like your favorite restaurant?***

And like your favorite restaurant my purpose is for you to be so outrageously happy with both the product and process – the complete experience – that you gladly introduce at least two people you care about to us before we sell your home…not because you feel obligated, but because you want the people you care about to have a great experience when they buy or sell a home, just like you have when you go to your favorite restaurant.

What you'll discover now is how to take this product and process pattern and make it a conversation so you're actually dialoguing with them about their favorite restaurant. The technique is called **morphing**.

You're going to get them to morph you to their favorite restaurant. As soon as they tell you what their favorite restaurant is you may decide to buy a certificate that entitles them to a free dinner every time they refer someone to you.

You get them completely morphed to that experience.

The reason you want to know their favorite restaurant is because most people have a place where they've experienced birthdays, anniversaries, weddings. They have special experiences they can remember and they spent time at that restaurant.

What you want to do is morph to that experience by saying, *"So for just a moment, can **you imagine that I am just like your favorite restaurant**?"*

***Exact Ways to Ask 13* – 6 Diamonds**
To see the video training in the
Magic Words Dojo for this dialogue, go to:
www.byreferralonly.com/WayToAsk13
(you will need to be logged in)

Exact Way to Ask 14

How to Use Confusion to Your Advantage

When you say something, it's selling.

When they say something, it's informing.

And when you quote someone who is quoting someone else, it's slightly confusing.

But that can be a good thing. Why?

Because the confusion embeds a suggestion that can go straight into the unconscious mind. This is called the Confusion Technique.

When a person is in a state of confusion, what they're looking for is one thought to grab onto they can understand.

Today we are in a marketplace where people are very confused and so you're going to use confusion to your advantage to encourage people to move in the direction of their dreams and goals:

"I was talking to a friend of mine who bought a house from me last year and she said that she was talking to a friend who also bought a home from me last year. And she told me my negotiating skills on loans are worth every penny that they paid for. Because of that, she's going to introduce me to the people who need my help."

The unconscious mind is more willing to hear a suggestion through a third voice than it is through the voice of the person who's speaking the words.

When I'm going to tell a story, I always say, *"Let me tell you what Jim McQuaid told me,"* or *"Let me tell you what I heard Terry Moerler say when I was at her office in Thousand Oaks and she was talking to a group of people. Listen to what she said."*

It's almost like you're observing a movie going on as opposed to listening to my words. Whatever I say next goes directly into the unconscious mind.

Whenever you're going to make an important point, find a second or third voice to put it in—a third voice will be very powerful—and then embed the command.

Here is a powerful way to do this.

When you talk about yourself, always use the voice of a happy client.

It does something really interesting for your psyche when you're thinking of a happy client. You think, *"What did that happy client say?"*

When you're at a listing presentation, you can say, *"Oh, here is what Mrs. Johnson said. She said..."*

Go ahead and make a list of all of your happy clients and find a quote they said to you. Then on your initial consultations, if you can put their words in your voice, it's going to be easier for your client to receive what you say than if it's coming directly from you.

I'll give you an example of saying what you want to say in a happy client's voice. It's really the root of referral mastery.

Imagine a prospect asks what makes you different than all the other agents.

"Well Mr. and Mrs. Prospect, the best way to do that is let me just tell you what Mr. Johnson said because he's like you and he wanted to get his home sold and he knows a lot of agents and lenders in the town and he said three things made a difference in his life to him about me. Let me tell you what he said the three things were.

He said, number one, my consulting skills. What he said is that I asked very profound, insightful questions.

The second thing he said was my negotiating skills. He said my negotiating skills alone were worth every penny that he paid me.

The third thing he said was my ability to organize all the transactional details. He said that because the transaction has hundreds of pieces of paper. He said he noticed how complex everything was. He counted 53 signatures on all the documents he had to sign and he said he was so delighted with how we took time with all of the details.

And you know what, I would have to agree with Mr. Johnson and say those are the three things that make the difference: our consulting, our negotiating, and our ability to oversee the transactional details."

You may notice it's easier to say and hear something when it's in Mr. Johnson's voice than when it is in your own voice.

When people can hear it from an objective outside voice, they start to witness it and feel like they're not trying to be persuaded. Instead, they're actually feeling informed, which is a totally different place to listen from.

When we're feeling that we're being persuaded, we listen differently than when we are being informed. The third person's voice makes us feel like we're being informed.

Oliver Wendell Holmes said, *"The mind, once expanded to a new dimension of a larger idea, never returns to its original size."*

How to Use Embedded Commands to Speak Directly to the Unconscious Mind!

An embedded command speaks directly to the unconscious mind.

It allows you to *influence* people to take a very specific action.

Embedded commands are one to four words that could stand alone outside the sentence you're saying. They make sense on their own.

"When I sat down with Mr. Johnson, he already knew about my consulting and negotiating skills. So he said to me, 'Let me just ***sign the listing contract****,' and I said, 'Well, let's do it,' and he did. So let's do it.* ***Let's sign the listing contract****."*

Can you see the embedded commands?

Sign the listing contract. Let's sign the listing contract.

Now listen to the embedded commands as you're sitting with a client:

"You know, Mr. and Mrs. Client, when I first sat down with Mr. and Mrs. Johnson they said to me, 'Hey Joe, I've already talked to Mr. and Mrs. Miller. They've told me all about your consulting and your negotiating and your overseeing the details and so I'm ***right now ready to sign*** *a listing contract,' and I said to him, 'Well, then let's* ***do it****,' and he reached over and he* ***signed the contract****. Now I'm not going to ask you* ***to sign the contract right now*** *because I haven't explained to you what I do, like what a consultant is, what a negotiator is, what a person who oversees the transactional details are, so I wouldn't ask you to do that right now."*

The bolded words are the embedded commands. I'm embedding the commands, *"Sign it. Sign the listing agreement. We'll be doing it* ***not*** *now, but we will be doing it."*

It's all going right past the conscious mind into the unconscious mind. It has to be spoken, because you can see that in writing it almost doesn't make sense. But spoken, it goes by them quickly, hypnotically. So when it's time for them to sign the listing contract, it's not the first time they heard the idea.

If you don't **practice daily**, you'll bumble and stumble through this. The embedded command is *"practice daily."*

When I'm coaching you I'll say to you, *"Embed the command..."* and then I'll give you the words to say. The right way to say an embedded command is to do the following:

1. Pause right before you embed the command;

2. Go a little bit louder with the command;

3. Downswing on the command;

4. Pause after the command.

Remember the four things: pause, raise your voice, downswing like you're commanding them, and pause. Then finish the rest of your statement.

So instead of saying...

"I want you to feel comfortable introducing me to your dear friends."

You would say...

*"I want you to...**FEEL comfortable introducing me**... to your dear friends."*

The pauses are minimal. Unnoticeable.

Say these embedded commands aloud right now:

- If you don't **practice this daily**, you will stumble and bumble through it.

- I'm not asking you to **sign the contract** because you probably have more questions you want to get answered before you **sign the contract**.

I've come up with a list of 13 embedded commands that are worthwhile practicing.

1. Learn how to embed the words "Sign the contract."
2. Learn how to embed the words "Introduce me."
3. Learn how to embed the words "Feel comfortable introducing me."
4. Learn how to embed the words "Accept this offer."
5. Learn how to embed the words "Decide now."
6. Learn how to embed the words "Act now."
7. Learn how to embed the words "Do what I say."
8. Learn how to embed the words "Feel motivated."
9. Learn how to embed the words "Take action."
10. Learn how to embed the words "Believe me."
11. Learn how to embed the words "Sign this now."
12. Learn how to embed the words "Listen to me."
13. Learn how to embed the words "Be comfortable."

Your job is to learn how to pause when you see those words, raise your voice, direct it as a command, and then pause after that.

Learn how to bombard people with embedded commands within any normal conversation.

Be constantly bombarding people with the outcome that you want from your communication.

The best way to do this when you go into a situation is to ask yourself, *"What do I want the outcome to be?"*

Put the answer into one to four words: *Sign the agreement. Introduce me. Decide now.*

What do you want the specific outcome to be?

If I'm working with a buyer and I want them to *decide now*, I'll be talking all about "deciding now."

I may get in the car with them and say, "*You know this morning I got to the office and the first thing I had to* ***decide*** *was which homes we're going to look at first."*

I may use the word "decide" over and over again in conversation so their unconscious mind is becoming very familiar with it. Then when I come to the right moment I say, *"Well, it's now time to* ***decide*** *which home you're going to own.*"

And now it's not the first time they're hearing it. Their unconscious mind is preparing for it the entire time.

That's what persuasion is. Persuasion is a gradual process of helping people become familiar with the unfamiliar, because it's unfamiliar for people to decide something this big. It's not something they do every day.

You start talking about deciding as if it's a way of life. You may come up with 20 stories about how you made decisions and watched other people make a decision. It could be something like:

"Hey, my daughter the other day she had to 'decide' where she was going to put her son in school." Again you've embedded the word decide.

When you're **learning new skills** like this, and every one can **learn new skills**, I believe that you have the capacity to understand concepts like the embedded command and that if you're willing to **practice them daily**, you'll feel much more comfortable; and if you choose not to **practice them daily**, you're going to stumble and bumble through these.

Imagine me saying this now. As I come to the embedded command, I pause, raise my voice, downswing on the command, and pause again before continuing.

Try reading it aloud.

***Exact Ways to Ask 14* – 7 Diamonds**
To see the video training in the
Magic Words Dojo for this dialogue, go to:
www.byreferralonly.com/WayToAsk14
(you will need to be logged in)

Exact Way to Ask 15

Get a Referral from those Who Are Easiest to Get It From!

50% of all the people who refer one person will refer a second person to you if you do a good job.

So if you do a really good job with somebody's referral, there's a good chance that person is going to recommend or introduce you to another person.

In fact, it's easier for a person to recommend a second person to you than it is the first, because you now have a track record with them. And they know how to do it.

Think of all those people who have referred one person to you. Now use this dialogue:

"Hello, Bob? I just want to thank you for introducing me to Larry. He told me that he shared with you what a great job that I did for him. Is that true?"

That's looking for compliance. Bob says, *"Yeah, that's true; I did tell him that."*

"Well, I heard a man named Joe Stumpf who is the founder of a company called 'By Referral Only' say that when a client refers you to a person and you do a great job for them, there's a 50% chance that they will introduce you to another person and I'm curious, Bob, do you think that's true?"

There are lots of delicious things happening in that dialogue!

First, you're acknowledging and thanking Bob for referring Larry, and then you're reminding him that Larry said you did a good job.

Then you're using an embedded command inside a quote. *"A guy named Joe Stumpf who owns this company called 'By Referral Only,' and here's what he says."* And you already know people listen differently when it's a third voice.

"A guy named Joe Stumpf owns this company called 'By Referral Only,' and here's what he said. He said that when you refer someone and you do a really good job, there's a 50% chance that you'll introduce a second person to him. Do you think that's true? Like is he telling the truth?"

It's a curious way of asking because if people go, *"Yes, I'd probably refer someone to you,"* they are answering the question that the unconscious mind is hearing. They may respond saying, *"Yes, I'd refer somebody if I know anybody."*

"*Well, the next time you're in a conversation with the person and he mentions he'd like to have a larger, more spacious home, right now, people who are selling their first home can move into a big home and get a big discount and buy a big house for a lot less than they ever could. Make sure you take your cell phone out, look up my number and call me immediately."*

It's a great way to introduce the concept of referring a second person to you.

***Exact Ways to Ask 15* – 10 Diamonds**
To see the video training in the
Magic Words Dojo for this dialogue, go to:
www.byreferralonly.com/WayToAsk15
(you will need to be logged in)

Exact Way to Ask 16

How to Get Your Top Inactive Referral Prospects to Introduce You

This is a wonderful script for when people you've been communicating with constantly don't introduce people to you.

You know they have the capacity, the influence, and the connections...

But they're still not introducing people to you!

Your dialogue would go like this:

"Hey Linda, I know that you're really busy and I also know you're the sort of person that goes out of their way to introduce your friends to a person that you really believe in. Don't you? And I'm curious. Do you believe in me enough to introduce me to the people that you really care about?"

Here's what to do if they say yes:

"Well now if you were me, what would you do to go about introducing me to the people that you think are most likely to need my help?"

If they're not referring people to you, it's important to check to see if they believe in you. You might find out some truths.

It's an evocative statement to say, *"I know that you're really busy and I also know that you're the sort of person that really goes out of their way to introduce your friends to the person that you really believe in and I'm curious do you believe in me enough to want to introduce me to the people you care about?"*

When you start this dialogue and you haven't talked to the person in a while, start by acknowledging that they're busy. *"I know you're busy so I'll keep it brief."*

DON'T start out with: *"Do you have time to talk?"*

DON'T ask if they're busy. Just assume they are.

Let's say you bump into a person you know at the store and they are the type of person who has not referred anyone to you, but you know they have the influence.

"Hey, I know you guys are really busy and I also know you're the kind of person that when it's time, you do go way out of your way to introduce friends and colleagues to people that you really believe in."

Then touch your chest! It's an embedded command that you really believe in yourself.

"And I'm curious. Do you believe in me enough to introduce me to the people that you care about?"

It takes courage to ask that question.

In my experience most people are not challenged in that way very often, so it really makes them look inside and go, *"Yes. Well I believe in you enough. I just don't know anyone."*

You have to be prepared for the answer, ready to take them to the next step:

"*Well if you were me then, what would you do to go about introducing me to the people that you think are most likely to need my help?*

I love that statement, *"If you were me."* It's a reversal and if you say it slowly…it causes the person to move out of their role into your role and think from your perspective. Many times they'll give you a pretty interesting answer.

If you follow this dialogue it will generate a referral conversation.

It's also okay to say things like, *"Hey, if you were me, what would you do to introduce people to me that needed my help? Do you have time right now? We can brainstorm this, talk a little bit about different ways that you can let the people that you really care about know that you're one of my clients."*

Inactive referrers just need a boost in conversation.

I was with Tom Cook in Canada at the Strategic Forum and we're getting ready to do a Main Event. As I was talking to Tom I realized he had not referred anyone to me in a while.

So I approached him and I said, "*Hey Tom, do you believe in us enough to introduce us to people when we come up to Toronto?"*

He said, *"Oh absolutely."*

I said, *"Well, so if you were me and you owned my company and you are bringing the Main Event up to Toronto, what would you do to make sure people were introduced to us?"*

And he said, *"God, I'd do a lot of things."*

I said, *"Well could we brainstorm for about 20 minutes right now about different ways to get people to the Main Event when we get up in Toronto?"*

It's a great dialogue when you know people believe in you.

"Do you believe in me enough that you'd want to introduce the people that you care about?"

When they say, *"Of course I do,"* it gives you an opportunity to make them more active. *"Great. Then let's talk about how to do that."*

Sometimes it's not about asking for a referral. Sometimes it's making suggestions about how people can refer others to you.

Sometimes you just need a good healthy discussion about ways to do it—what we can do at your work, what we can do at your church, what we can do with your family, what we do in your neighborhood, how we could refer some of the people that were at your wedding.

For example: *"I know that you had a baptism at your house a couple of months ago and I know that you have an older daughter. What could we do to talk about the ways you can let the people that you really care about know that I'm your agent and you're my client?"*

Sometimes that's what it takes. If people believe in you, they'll have that conversation.

***Exact Ways to Ask 16* – A Diamonds**
To see the video training in the
Magic Words Dojo for this dialogue, go to:
www.byreferralonly.com/WayToAsk16
(you will need to be logged in)

Exact Way to Ask 17

How to Know with 100% Certainty If the Person You Are Talking to Will Ever Introduce You!

When you want to discover if people are the type to refer you, the dialogue would go like this:

"Joe Stumpf, the founder of By Referral Only, said when it comes to referrals the population is divided into three groups. He said that 15% of the people will refer me without even asking. 15% won't refer me because they don't promote under any circumstances. 70% of the people will refer if I ask them in an intelligent way. I was wondering what group do you think you fall into?"

It's a great dialogue in an initial consultation just to open up the conversation around referrals. Even if you've already said your purpose in your initial consultation, you can say:

"My purpose is for you to be so outrageously happy with the help that I provide you that you would gladly introduce me to the people that you care about most. Even a guy named Joe Stumpf says that the population is divided into three groups. He said that 15% of the population ***will refer*** *when I do a good job for him. 15% will not refer no matter what I do because they don't promote anything, but 70% of the population will refer if I ask in an intelligent way. I'm curious. What group do you think you guys fall in to?"*

It's a great way to introduce the concept of referrals right up front.

It's also a great dialogue when you contact somebody who has never referred anyone to you, especially if you have been mailing the Evidence of Success, Letter from the Heart, and Newsletter, but you have never heard from them.

This might be a good call just to see if they're still qualified to be on the list. If I was ever going to clean out my database, just to see who's going to stay I might use this dialogue. I might even hire a telemarketer to use a dialogue like this:

"Hey, Mark. This is John Jones. I'm calling on behalf of Marge. Marge asked me just to give you a quick call and ask you a question."

"Well, what's up?"

"Well, you remember Marge. She was your real estate consultant seven years ago."

"Yes, I remember Marge."

"Well, she told me that there's a guy named Joe Stumpf," and go right into the dialogue. *"Marge was wondering, what group do you think you fall into?"*

You might want to take all the people who say they never refer anyone and just remove them from your database.

15% of people in our culture don't refer and you may be one of them for all I know. Ask yourself how active are you as an advocate for people or is it just not your nature?

Then there's 15% of population that doesn't need to do much to be an advocate. **You must be careful of building your business on that 15% alone, meaning that you can get too dependent on one or two people to do all of your referring in your business.**

If you do that, you have a one-legged business. I've seen agents who work with just one builder or mortgage officer who rely on one real estate agent for all their referrals. They become too dependent on one individual person.

The strongest business is the one based on the 70% of people who will advocate for you if you ask in an intelligent, articulate way.

You have to bombard that 70% with your embedded command. I say *bombard* because there are so many messages coming from people that are calling for their attention. They turn the TV on, read the newspaper, listen to radio. So many people are bombarding them with messages to "buy me, hire me."

The message that you have to send over and over again is, *"Who are you noticing? Are you thinking about me? What do I have to do to encourage you to recommend me?"*

Now when people say to you, "Well, yes. I think I'm in the 70% group. I would do it if I knew somebody and you ask me," you might say to them:

"Well, what stops you from introducing more people to me who need my help?"

Listen to the embedded command. *"What stops you from introducing me to more people who may need my help?"* In order for them to answer the question, they have to think about what they have to do to introduce you to more people.

Often people can answer that question better than, *"Who do you know that wants to buy their next house?"* because they can't think of an answer to that question.

They don't think, *"Well, I have a friend right now who I think is about to move out. I don't know how to introduce them to you,"* or, *"There are some people at work that are interested in talking, but I don't know how to..."* It's easier for them to tell you what's in the way of making it happen.

Like I might say to you, *"Hey. What stops you from introducing more people to By Referral Only?"* That might be easier for you to answer than, *"Who's the next person you know that would like to join the coaching program?"*

Suppose you say, *"Hey. What stops you from introducing more people?"* and they say, "Well, I don't know."

You say, *"Well, I'm curious. If you did know the answer to that question, what would the answer be?"*

Most people when they say *"I don't know"* are being numb. But there's something below numb. To find it, you can do this...

When someone at one of my trainings says, *"I don't know,"* I'll say:

"I know it's a difficult question that ***you're going to be answering****. The question I'm asking you is if you did know the answer, what would it be?"*

So you can say, *"Hey. What stops you from introducing me to more people that may need my help?"*

"I don't know."

"I know it's a difficult question. I'm curious if you did know, what do you think the answer would be?"

It just gives people a chance to explore it. I believe many more of your clients need more time dedicated to exploring how they can introduce people to you. This is not just a drive-by request.

A drive-by goes like this:

"Oh by the way, do you know anyone who wants to buy or sell?"

"I don't know anyone right now."

"Thanks for thinking about it. I'm curious, when you say you don't know anyone, is it that you don't know anyone right now or you don't know if you want to refer anyone to me?"

You help them get clarity. It creates bigger conversations.

You have more rapport with people than you believe you do.

You have more permission to do this than you may believe you do.

You may or may not treat the request for a referral with enough reverence. You may spend a ton of time designing an ad or creating your website or what goes into your direct mail pieces.

But when you treat a referral with reverence, then when you're with someone who likes you, knows you and trusts you, you will be proud to really explore what stops them and what's beyond, *"I just don't know."* You will really explore that with them.

When people say, *"I just don't know anyone."* You can even say:

"Are you sure?"

"Yes, I'm sure."

"*Are you sure enough to be unsure?"*

I love that thought. *Are you sure enough to be unsure?*

After they go into a slightly confused state, you can give attention and direction. It might sound like this:

"What do you mean?"

"Well, how would you know it's not true that you don't know anyone?"

"Well, I do know someone."

All you've done is just loosen the resistance and help them explore a little deeper.

Most people are walking around with the name of a referral on the tip of their tongue.

Here some additional little tricks that you could use...

When somebody says, *"I don't know if I want to buy a house,"* you could say:

"Are you sure?" That loosens it up.

"Well, yes. I'm pretty sure."

"Are you sure enough to be unsure?"

While they're in a state of confusion trying to figure out what you just said, you say, *"How would you know that's not true?"*

"Well, I don't have enough money to buy a house."

Now that's a different issue than *I don't want to buy a house.*

"*Oh. Let's explore the money then."* Now you're talking about something that's the real core issue.

The reason most people aren't referring people to you is they don't know how good it's going to feel when they do.

***Exact Ways to Ask 17* – J Diamonds**
To see the video training in the
Magic Words Dojo for this dialogue, go to:
www.byreferralonly.com/WayToAsk17
(you will need to be logged in)

Exact Way to Ask 18

The Dialogue You MUST Use before You EVER Talk about Your Compensation!

What do you do if someone asks how you're compensated?

The dialogue goes like this:

"First, I work on a contingent basis versus a retainer basis, which means as your consultant, negotiator and overseer of all the details, I invest all of the upfront money and time to help you make your dreams come true, and only when your dreams come true do I actually receive compensation. Then of course the second way you compensate me is in the form of your recommendations and introductions to your friends, family and neighbors that you care about. Does that make sense?"

It's a preemptive script. You'd be surprised that most people are not clear on compensation and when people are not clear on compensation they start negotiating it right away.

If clients don't know how you get paid, they're going to ask you to cut your pay. This dialogue is preemptive in that you must use it before you begin talking about compensation in order to cut off their lack of information.

Preemptive means you bring it up before the client does because you must know it's on everybody's mind.

So initially, you would say:

"You might be wondering right now how do I get paid? Well first I work on a contingent basis versus a retainer which means as your consultant, your negotiator and the person who oversees all the transactional details, I invest all the upfront money to help make your dreams come true and only

when your dreams come true do I actually receive compensation."

This part of the dialogue is called *reframing.*

You're taking the words *commission*, *contingent* and *retainer* and putting them in a new frame.

What does it mean to work on a commission basis?

What does it mean to work on a contingent basis?

What does it mean to work on a retainer basis?

You're introducing a different way of thinking about how you get paid.

When people hear *commission*, they think *"Will you cut it?"* In our culture, there's a lot of literature that's written on the whole concept of compensation. One of those things is that we are taught at a young age to negotiate commission. All commissions are negotiable.

Your parents told you that a long time ago. Car salespeople work on commission, so you can negotiate that deal. So when you say the word *commission*, you're introducing the idea of negotiating.

So I'm going to suggest that you remove the word commission and reframe it to say that you work on a *contingent* basis. You invest all the time, energy and effort and you only get paid when their dream comes true.

That's a really important concept for them to understand. If you put it inside that frame early, it gives more reverence for what you do.

You're taking the risk. *"I'm assuming the risk and I only get compensated when your dream comes true."*

Then when you say, *"And my compensation is,"* it's connected to their dream coming true, not what they can negotiate with you. It happens very subtly, but very powerfully.

How to Use a "Selfish" Benefit to Really Connect

After you explain your contingent compensation, you ask what I call a "Selfish Benefit" question:

"And the most time-consuming part of any transaction is looking for new clients and how would you rather I spend my time—out looking for new clients or serving your needs?"

These two dialogues connect well together. You talk to them about introducing people that they care about so you can spend more time, energy and effort helping make their dream come true rather than having to look for new clients.

It's really important that you say this in a neutral way. State it as a matter of fact. You're not defending it. You're not getting charged up about it.

You're just saying:

"You know, Mr. and Mrs. Client, right now if I were you I'd probably be sitting there right now saying, 'Hey, how does this guy get compensated?' Well, let me explain. Here are the facts: first, I work on a contingent basis and what that means is I invest all the upfront money. Not a retainer. You're not going to give me any money tonight. Whew, good news, huh? You won't be writing a check tonight. You'll only compensate me if your dreams come true. That's how I get compensated."

So you're creating that concept, and then you're connecting it to:

"Then of course the second way you compensate me is in the form of recommendations and introductions to your friends, your family members and your neighbors and the people that you care about. Does that make sense?"

There's such a beautiful connection when you can say, *"Then of course. Then of course. Then of course."*

When people ask what your commission is, you say, *"I work on a contingent basis, and that means I invest all the upfront money. I pay for the marketing, the advertising, all the exposure on your home and assume all of the risks, and only when I make your dream come true do I get compensated, and the way I get compensated is on a formula based on the sales price multiplied by 2.5%."*

When we get into compensation, I love using a visual. Take out six $1.00 bills and just lay them on the table and say:

"Let me show you how all this gets divided."

Separate three dollars and say, *"That goes to the selling broker."*

Take the other three and say, *"This comes to our brokerage house. Let me just show you what happens to these three. This one goes over here to my broker. This one goes for expenses in running my business. This last one is profit. How much of my profit do you want from my dollar?"*

You're planting the idea that people would have to take your last dollar.

So you can literally say, *"Are you going to take my last dollar?"*

Most of the time, it's not even necessary to go there. They get that you are taking the biggest risk and it helps to add that the second way you get compensated is by recommendations and introductions to the people they care about most. The implication is that you're worth even more.

It's all preemptive.

It's all stated with a neutral charge, meaning "this is just the way it is" and it eliminates any future conversation about your value or the idea that you might cut your commission.

***Exact Ways to Ask 18* – 3 Hearts**
To see the video training in the
Magic Words Dojo for this dialogue, go to:
www.byreferralonly.com/WayToAsk18
(you will need to be logged in)

Exact Way to Ask 19

Master the Art of Showing Clients the Selfish Benefit They Get for Referring You!

People want to know the big benefit to them if they introduce people to you.

One of the things you always want to avoid at all costs is a conversation about, "Will you pay me to refer you people?"

So here's how the dialogue goes:

"You know Mr. and Mrs. Client, there is another benefit for you introducing me to your friends during your transaction that you may or may not already be aware of. See Mr. and Mrs. Client, you probably already know that the most time-consuming part of any business is finding new clients, and what I would like to suggest is in the days and weeks ahead, when you have sold your home/gotten your loan/bought your home, you will look back and feel great that you introduced me to your friends during the transaction, because it allowed me to invest the maximum amount of time, energy and resources into you rather than looking for new clients."

The worst thing that can happen is professionals get into this habit of saying, *"Oh, yes, I'll give you a referral fee."* Then the person who they refer now wants a referral fee if they refer anyone to you. Then the next person, and so on, and on.

You cannot give to one person what you can't give to everybody, because the worst thing that can happen is if somebody refers and they find out you paid someone else to get a referral, but didn't pay them.

If anything goes wrong and you paid someone for the referral, it's a dirty profit—like I got paid a referral fee, and then you bought a house, but it got all messed up, but I still got paid. It gets real messy.

So one of the things that you say to people is:

"There's a real big benefit that you may or may not be aware of when you refer and you may not know, but the biggest time-consuming part of any transaction is finding new clients. In the days and weeks ahead, when you've sold your home/you've gotten your loan, and you look back and you feel really great that the introductions to your friends and your family members allowed me to invest more time and energy and resources into helping you rather than look for new clients, and that's the essence of it—that you really have a choice. I'm going to look for new clients and you could either introduce them to me, or I can go out and find them on my own. If I go out and find them on my own, I have to take time, energy and effort away from you, but if you introduce them to me, you're going to feel great because I'll be able to spend more time with you, and that's the big selfish benefit."

There are two language patterns here that you want to notice and you might want to underline.

"*You may or may not.*"

When you say, *"You may or may not,"* it's like saying, *"I'm not saying you will, I'm just saying you may or may not."* Right after saying that, it's easy to embed a command:

"You may or may not ***sign the listing*** *agreement tonight, you'll make that decision a little bit later."*

"You may or may not ***introduce me*** *to the people that you care about."*

"You may or may not" softens things before you give the command.

You may or may not **learn these patterns** in many different ways.

You may or may not **practice these all next week.**

You may or you may not **rewrite the language pattern**.

Another pattern you want to look at is using the word *suggestion*.

"I would like to suggest..."

In the initial consultation, you will hear me say:

"I'd like to suggest that in the days and weeks ahead, you will come to really appreciate that I'm the person who oversees all your transactional details."

This is another way of saying I don't know exactly when, but it's very plausible that you will sign a listing agreement. It's very ambiguous.

It's not setting a timeline, but it's very plausible that you're going to come to this conclusion and so the unconscious mind can agree with that.

In the days and weeks ahead, you will find real value in having **practiced** these Magic Words language patterns diligently and it will become apparent too that it was worth every minute of it.

I'm saying to you, this is what's going to happen in the future, but I'm not saying you're going to do it. I'm just saying you're going to come to see that when you diligently practice these Magic Words language patterns, you're going to feel really good.

It's all going into your unconscious mind right now.

Exact Ways to Ask 19 **– 4 Hearts**
To see the video training in the
Magic Words Dojo for this dialogue, go to:
www.byreferralonly.com/WayToAsk19
(you will need to be logged in)

Exact Way to Ask 20

How to Make Someone Comfortable with a Future Pacing Question

When you ask a future pacing question, you may discover that people will tell you what they need in order to get comfortable.

This is great because if they don't feel comfortable giving you a referral, then we need to have a conversation about that.

What is the unconscious reason they're not comfortable?

There can be a whole variety of reasons why they're not comfortable, so using these Magic Words can help you discover what's causing the discomfort.

It sounds like this:

*"Hey Barbara, first of all I'd like to say thank you for **trusting me** enough to be honest with me. Second I'd like to ask what happens when you imagine a family member, a friend or a neighbor calling you with total gratitude because they just sold their home/bought a home/got a loan and you know that the tremendous value and advice they received was all due to you introducing them to me so that I could help them?"*

Now, that's such a powerful dialog because you're taking the focus off of them being uncomfortable referring you, and focusing on how they're going to feel when the person they refer gets the value you're going to provide for them.

The number one reason people refer—you know this—is to feel good. **You've got to keep on reminding people that when they refer friends, their friends are going to feel good.**

There are a couple of things going on inside that dialog. There's a powerful embedded command called "trust me." You can hear it in: *"First, I'd like to say thank you for* ***trusting me****."* As I've done in the other dialogs, you can anchor this with your tone of voice and with a hand gesture. You can reach out and touch them as you say, *"Thank you for trusting me."*

That's very powerful. When you use the word trust in this way, you're not saying "trust me," you're saying, *"Thank you for trusting me enough to be honest with me."*

In order to understand what you're going to say next, you have to get them to start imagining.

"Well, what happens when you imagine a family member, or a friend or a neighbor calling you with total gratitude because they just told you their home was sold, and you know the tremendous value and advice they received was all due to you introducing them to me so that I could help them?"

Everything after the word "because" becomes three times stronger. What you want people to do is create a mental movie of what happens. You can say:

"What happens when I imagine my friend calling me up and just completely being grateful for all the value they just received and it's all because I introduced them and they were able to get help? What does that feel like?"

They say, *"It feels good."*

"Who's the next person you know that's most likely to do what you just did? You guys bought your first home. You were living in an apartment. You weren't certain what to do next, and then you got the advice and now today, as a result, you got into a home with no down payment and house payment equivalent in what you're paying in rent, and I know you know someone. It could be your brother, your sister, it could be your cousin who's also renting an apartment, or

could be somebody from your apartment that you lived in, or it even could be somebody from work. You told me somebody at JB Electronics was going to be moving into a house soon or it could be somebody from your church. I know you know somebody. Right now, who comes to mind first?"

Now you're asking people for a referral from a place where they feel comfortable, and that's the secret.

You always want to make sure that when somebody expresses their discomfort, that you first get them into a place where they're feeling comfortable. Then ask them once they're already in that state of being comfortable.

Here's How to Make Them Feel Good before You Even Ask for the Referral!

You can anchor a good feeling before you actually ask someone to refer you.

What you DON'T want to do is this:

"Hey, would you be comfortable referring your friends or family members to me?"

"I don't know, it all depends."

"Well, who's the next person you know?"

Can you see why this is wrong? You're asking them when they've already told you they're not comfortable.

You always want to ask people for a referral after you've anchored them in comfort.

Here's how...

"Imagine what it's going to feel like when the agents who come to the Main Event Masters after you've introduced them to us, call you up after the event? Imagine this...

They're calling you on their cell phone. They're on their way home and they go, 'Hey, I've just come back from the Main Event Masters. Thank you so much for introducing Joe Stumpf to us. If it wasn't for you, I would've never come to the event.'

Now imagine what that's going to feel like knowing they've received all the value from the event only because you were willing to introduce them, and then we were able to help them?"

Now, who is the next person you know that would most likely need to get the kind of coaching and advice we can give them at the Main Event Masters?"

You see how this works? You're only asking after you create an anchor so that they're thinking about what it will be like *after* they've referred someone to you—and that's called **future pacing**.

Future pacing gets people to experience what you want the outcome to be by asking them to step into that outcome.

You also want to make sure they are not disassociated from the referral.

"Hey, what's it going to be like? I mean just imagine. Imagine what it's going to feel like for you and what it's going to be like for you when a friend of yours calls you up and says 'Thank you so much for introducing me to Joe,' and they're just filled with gratitude because they were able to buy their first home which they would've never been able to buy if you didn't introduce them to me? Imagine what that's going to feel like."

They're going to be disassociated from this dialogue, watching it from a distance like a movie until you associate it directly with them:

"I wonder who is the next person you know that you would love to make sure is able to get their first home and they need advice, and you want them to call you up someday and thank you for introducing them to me so they could get their own home?"

Now you've **associated** them directly with the referral. That's how the mind works both at the conscious and unconscious level, so when you're in a conversation with a person asking them and you're saying:

"I'm curious. You say you're not comfortable referring people to me. I'm really grateful that you can even trust me to be honest with me. Secondly, I'm just really wondering what happens when you imagine a really good friend of yours or a family member of yours calling you up and expressing a tremendous amount of gratitude because they were able to buy their first home or move up to a larger, more spacious home, all because you introduced them to me so I could help them? What does that feel like?"

They say, *"That feels pretty good."*

But really...they don't even have to answer.

The unconscious mind is doing it all for them already. Just roll on and say:

"Because I want to feel good and I know you want to help the people that you care about. I'm curious, who is the next person you know that's most likely to do what you just did?"

Then go on to making your request.

This contains more advanced language skills, but whenever you get into that place where somebody says they're uncomfortable—and in the past you might have said, *"Well, thanks anyway"*—you can now help them become comfortable as opposed to allowing them to stay in their discomfort.

That's important, because if you walk away and they're still uncomfortable, it's very hard for you to come back in the future and start up a conversation. That's because your mind is saying: *"Now they're uncomfortable referring people. They don't want to refer anyone to me."*

You might as well learn how to deal with people's discomfort. It will occur from time to time, so being able to access this skill whenever discomfort comes up in your clients is going to help.

***Exact Ways to Ask 20* – 9 Hearts**
To see the video training in the
Magic Words Dojo for this dialogue, go to:
www.byreferralonly.com/WayToAsk20
(you will need to be logged in)

Exact Way to Ask 21

Use This Simple Dialogue at a Party to Let Everyone Know Who You Are

What do you say at a party when someone comes up to and asks, *"Hey, what's your connection here to the party?"*

"Well, I'm John Jones. Sandy Collins and Bob Collins are my ideal clients. Let me tell you what it's like to be their real estate or mortgage consultant. Sandy and Bob are some of the friendliest, most authentic people that I've had the privilege to consult with and negotiate for. All throughout the process of helping them buy this beautiful home they were willing to answer some real thought-provoking questions, so that I could take the time to really craft the strategy to help them figure out what was important to them. Bob and Sandy trusted my advice and today they are comfortable recommending me to the people that they care about most."

Once you look closely at this dialogue the key words you're embedding are "my ideal client."

Imagine if you had an opportunity to talk to everybody at that party, what would you want to say? By the time the party was over, you'd ideally want everyone at the party to know that the person throwing the party is your client.

You would walk around and introduce yourself as the person who helped Bob and Sandy buy their home and describe them as your ideal client. **The reason that's so powerful is there so much congruency and social proof**.

Dr. Cialdini talks about social proof in his discussion of the hierarchy of influence. While *reciprocity* is the most powerful way of influencing people, the second most useful and powerful way to influence people is through social proof.

My definition of social proof is *proof* which pressures people to conform.

There have been a lot of experiments performed on what social proof is. For example, a study done in New York had someone stand at a busy intersection and look up at the sky for 60 seconds. They counted the number of people who walked by in that 60 seconds who also looked up. They discovered less than 2% of the people would mimic what one person was doing.

Then they had four of the people standing at the same corner and look up. Within 60 seconds, 75% of the people walking past, stopped and looked up.

What the research says is that people don't mirror what one person is doing. They look to see what a group of people are doing.

There's a young lady that does a lot of work for the Home Shopping Network. She's a masterful copywriter who improved their sales by 17%. She simply changed a couple of words, and the call to action. At one time, the Home Shopping Network said, *"Operators are standing by. Call now."* She changed the words to, *"If operators are busy, please call back later."*

Sales improved significantly with just that little shift in words. Why?

Because for the person who is unsure about buying, they experience that everyone else is doing it. Just the thought that the number may be busy means that other people are doing it.

If you've ever watched a Jerry Lewis' telethon, they always have the people visible in the background answering phones so you can see the phones ringing. They've proven over and over again that when people see and hear the phones ringing, all the others start to ring right after. When there's a silence, silence continues. In most cases they now rig the phone to ring, just to get the ball rolling.

When people are uncertain what to do, they look to see what everyone else is doing. That's social proof.

We experience it in our business at By Referral Only. At our events, we watch how people sign up because everyone else is signing up. If others are doing it, it must be good. It must be the right thing to do.

In your communications you could say, *"So far this year, 1,183,416 people have bought their first home. Is it time for you to take advantage like a million other people have across this country of low prices and own your own home?"*

Now you're using social proof, saying millions of people are doing it. You're not saying first time home sales are down by 40% in our area which is the reverse of social proof. That's part of the tragedy of the mass media. They talk in terms of reverse social proof. They say, *"In Thousand Oaks, foreclosures are up 730%."* They go for the shock factor. They don't say, *"Foreclosures went from 53 to 187." They say "up by 730%."* They use a number that freezes everybody.

The opposite of that would be, *"This month 473,217 people made their house payment on time."* That would be social proof.

The more you can show that other people are doing what you're asking them to do, the more likely others will follow. That's why whenever you're in a social setting, let as many people as possible know that the person at that party who's having that event is your client—not that you're their real estate agent.

You don't want to be promoting yourself as the real estate agent. You want to be promoting yourself as, *"They're my client."*

Does that make sense to you, that distinction there? That's social proof. If everyone at the party knows that they've picked me, others will pick me, too.

It's been proven over and over again that canned laughter, even if what's being shown isn't funny, will make people laugh harder than something that's really funny, but lacks canned laughter.

We go along with the crowd. It's just innate in us. That's who we are. When we're uncertain what to do next, we look to see what everyone else is doing.

So when you're at a party or a social gathering, people are unsure what to talk about until you create the conversation. The conversation is that they're your ideal client and you talk about them in terms of your ideal client.

You can even offer a toast:

"I'd like to toast John and Sandy because they've been my ideal client. When I was helping them get this home, these folks allowed me to ask them some really thought-provoking questions. They allowed me to really consult and negotiate for them. I tell you these are the best type of people you're ever going to work with. These are the ideal people to work with."

You're talking about yourself, but you're talking about them in regards to you. So whenever you get that chance to make a conversation in a social setting, you're giving other people permission to put themselves into a position to want to be an ideal client too.

They don't want you to be their real estate agent. They want to be your ideal client.

You hear that distinction? That's the social proof that you want.

"*See, John? He's one of my ideal clients. There's Betty, one of my ideal clients, and Larry over there, he's one of my ideal clients.*"

Refer to everybody as your ideal client so you're not the real estate agent. That's where that shift starts to occur where you can get a lot more social proof.

Exact Ways to Ask 21 **– Q Hearts**
To see the video training in the
Magic Words Dojo for this dialogue, go to:
www.byreferralonly.com/WayToAsk21
(you will need to be logged in)

Exact Way to Ask 22

Use Six Degrees of Separation to Generate Infinite Numbers of Referrals!

Here's another strong way to ask for referrals:

"Who is the next person you know that's most likely to do what you just did?" Then describe in great detail specifically what you did for the client. Then you say, *"I know you know someone. It may be a person in your family. It may be a friend or a neighbor. It may be a person from your church. It may someone from work. By now, I know you know someone. I'm curious who comes to mind first."*

That's such a strong dialogue.

One of the things I've learned is never underestimate the depth of the pool that people swim in. In a typical base of 150 people—your top 150—the number of possible referrals and introductions that can be created with all the possible contacts within six degrees of separation is almost incalculable.

Todd Welsh was sharing with me that he was with one of his top 150 people. The guy mentioned to him that he was going to go up to a Blue Jays game. He's in Salina, Kansas. The Blue Jays are the Kansas team.

He said, *"Gosh. I've never been to a Blue Jays game before."*

His friend said, *"You ought to come with us. We're all getting out on a bus. We're taking the bus up there, a bunch of my friends."*

So Todd got on the bus. He met 30 people on the bus that this guy knew very well. Over the last year, he's helped 9 out of those 30 people as a direct result of the bus ride from Salina to Kansas.

If you were to meet each person you work with and just draw a circle and say, *"Everybody has an inner circle,"* you'd come up with maybe a dozen people for each person. It could be your disciples. It could be the people that are closest to you, your family and friends.

Then draw another circle around that inner circle and point out, *"Then there's a group of people at work, people at church, people in your social networks."* Then draw another circle around that. That's where you start to go out to their chiropractor, to their dentist, to the people that are their vendors and their suppliers. Then you go out another circle and those are their acquaintances.

Never underestimate the levels of which people can connect you. Have you have heard about the Six Degrees of Separation? That's where we're all connected to anyone else in our community—some say the world—by just six relationships in some way or another.

When you're asking people who the next person they know is—the most likely to do what they just did—it might not be someone they know, but someone they introduce us to might know someone. That's what you're really looking at. You're looking at those degrees of separation. They don't know if Bob, their chiropractor, is going to buy or sell, but they're happy to introduce you to Bob.

Here's a great exercise:

1. Right now write down the names of three people who have introduced and referred someone to you in the last 90 days.

2. Now ask the question, "How did they refer you and how were they related to the person that they referred?"

3. What was the process by which they introduced you or referred you?

4. How did you connect with that person?

5. How are they related to that person?

Now when you're asking for a referral, you can actually use those as case studies to show social proof. Say:

"Who is the next person you know that's most likely to do what you just did? You guys just bought your first house. You lived in an apartment. Now you own a home of your own. as a matter of fact, friends of mine who I just helped buy their first home, they were living in Oakwood Garden apartments. They bought a three-bedroom, two-bath home over on Hiawatha Street. They introduced me to their sister who has a friend at work who wanted to buy their first home. I've been able to help them."

If you can give short case studies—evidence of success—about how you've helped other people refer you, most people can find themselves in the story. They can find ways that they can help you if they can hear how other people are helping you.

Your clients are thinking, *"The more that you can give me examples of how other people are helping you, the easier it is for me to help you."*

When you're asking people, *"Who do you know,"* you're thinking beyond just the center of influence they know directly. You're trying to get them to expand out further to their church, to their work, to friends of friends, to family members, to uncles. Keep stretching them out.

Avoid this Critical Mistake

The biggest mistake that you could make is having a sense of entitlement when you ask, as opposed to asking only for an introduction.

I hear people say, *"Hey. Now that I've helped you buy a house, you've got to replace yourself."* That's a sense of entitlement, as opposed to saying, "*I'm not asking you to refer someone to me. All I'm asking you to do is introduce me to people and I'll talk to them. I'll find out how I could be of great value to them.*"

Most people, and you know this in your own experience, will do more for simple recognition than they will do for money. People refer because they want to feel good.

Rupert Murdock has certain rules that he applies to all his local newspapers. One of the rules is that 80% of the news in his small-town papers must contain a picture of someone who lives locally in that area, because he knows that people read local newspapers to find out about the local people.

The more you use people's names in your newsletters, the more you use pictures of your clients, the more you have a "client of the month" recognition, client birthdays and drop client names, the more you will be referred or introduced.

Never underestimate how likely people are to show someone that their name appeared in your newsletter. People get a warm feeling when they see themselves in print.

It's very powerful when you understand the concept of knowing that when a person's name is highlighted somewhere, they go out of their way to show people their name. The more you do that in all of your marketing, the more you'll be introduced to a wider range of people.

***Exact Ways to Ask 22* – J Hearts**
To see the video training in the
Magic Words Dojo for this dialogue, go to:
www.byreferralonly.com/WayToAsk22
(you will need to be logged in)

Exact Way to Ask 23

Don't Ask for NEW Referrals; Be Grateful for the Ones You Already Have

You get whatever you're grateful for.

Suppose I'm calling one of the clients that referred someone to us, and then I'm going to call all the way through the entire chain of everyone who's linked to that referral.

So the first call would go to Bob, and I would say, *"Hey, Bob, thank you for introducing me to Larry. I met with him and he's chosen to work with me and I will make sure that Larry is delighted that you introduced me and I'll keep you posted on our progress. Thanks."*

I hang up, then call up Mary who's connected to Bob. *"Mary, I just met with Larry and he chose to work with me and the reason I'm telling you this is because Bob introduced him to me so thank you for introducing Bob to me because without him, I would've never met Larry."*

Whatever you're grateful for, you get more of!

This is one of the most powerful things we teach at By Referral Only. So instead of calling and asking for referrals, call and be grateful for the referrals that you've already gotten.

It seems to me that *grateful* is more important than saying, "Thank you." Being grateful is more of a spiritual experience for people than it is a personal experience. So when I really experience some of this gratitude, there's a spiritual quality to that.

Eric Hoffer said, *"The hardest arithmetic to master is that which enables us to count our blessings."*

Let people know how their behavior eight years ago is affecting you today when you call all the way up your chain.

You know Bob, Mary, Tom, Susan, Kevin, and Ron. Right now you're talking to Ron and saying, *"Ron, we met nine years ago and today I'm meeting with a young family that's going to be buying their first home that I would've never ever had the opportunity to serve if you wouldn't have taken the time to refer Susan to me that afternoon and as a result. I'm now working with this family. I'm just so blessed and so grateful for that."*

What I've known in my life is that the more I express my gratitude, the more I get what I'm expressing my gratitude for. The more I'm in fear of what I'm not getting, I start asking for what I want and the more that I'm pressuring people for what I want, the less I get because I'm not grateful for what I already have.

How to Manage Your Client List to Make Money from Every Relationship

If you look in your My Clients referral management system, we use the whole Referral Tree feature there and you can organize and account for all of your past clients right in My Client.

The secret to the referral chain is really being able to manage all of this.

When you go into My Client you can use the Lifetime Value function to monetize every relationship. You can look at every person you've ever worked with and know what each person's lifetime value is.

Another feature of My Client is the ability to use a direct referral function where you can trace the lineage and what happens with each introduction. This allows you to know the number of people who are talking about you versus just how many of them are converting.

If you see you're getting lots of referrals, but it's not translating into money, you know the skill you have to work on after you get the name is following through to get an appointment.

You need to be more skilled on the initial consultation, and then using the All Referral function. It gives you the big picture view of all the referral activity that's going on in your business, and this number tells you how active your base is.

Some people have said, *"Yes, I've got 100% referral business."*

I will say, *"That's interesting. Let me see what that looks like,"* and they have four people referring eight or nine people a year to them. That's not a very active referral business. If anything happens to any of those four people, the agent doesn't have a business any more.

You need to look at all these functions:

What's the lifetime value of each client and do you know what those numbers are and what all the connections are?

How many direct referrals do you have? That tells you how well you're converting the number of people who are being referred to you.

What are your total referrals? That tells you how active your base is.

You're trying to improve on all three areas. You're trying to improve *the lifetime value* of each client, *the number of referrals that convert* to business, and to *get more people referring* people to you.

It's better to have a few referrals from a lot of people than a lot of referrals from a handful of people. It's just a more stable business and a more predictable outcome.

You can sit down and update everybody on your referral tree even if there's no activity. You can call to say,

"Hey, there are no branches growing right now. Maybe you want to start another tree?"

The biggest part about that is the idea that gratitude can make a day and change a life. All that's necessary is your willingness to put it into words. You could be super grateful, but if you're not expressing it to people, they don't know it.

To express your gratitude over and over to people is just to encourage them to behave in a way that enables them to receive more gratitude.

So if you call your client base and tell them what their behavior is doing today based on referrals they made years ago, and they're hearing that all the time, all they want to do is give you more referrals so they can continue to hear more of your gratitude.

We love to feel appreciated.

***Exact Ways to Ask 23* – 4 Spades**
To see the video training in the
Magic Words Dojo for this dialogue, go to:
www.byreferralonly.com/WayToAsk23
(you will need to be logged in)

Exact Way to Ask 24

Discover the Most Powerful Analogy that Will Make It Easier for Your Client to Refer You!

When physicist Niels Bohr was describing the solar system, he used the metaphor of atoms circling a neuron. He was trying to make a word picture:

"If you want to look at molecular structure, it's just like the solar system. It's just like..."

When you hear the word "like" it's usually an analogy and it's easier to enter into the unconscious mind.

"I'm like a general contractor for your business. What I'm doing is using words as a tool to help you increase your income."

Instead of simply saying, *"I'm a business coach,"* I used an analogy comparing myself to a general contractor, but referring to your business instead of a house. My tools are words to help you construct systems and processes that help you make more money.

Creating analogies helps you create word pictures in people's minds so they can connect the dots quickly.

Here is the dialogue:

"As your real estate/mortgage consultant, I am like the pilot of your plane. My role is to get you where you want to go, safe and on time. Because I count on you to introduce me to the people that you care about, would you do me a favor?"

"Oh, yes. What is that, Joe?"

"During the transaction, as I deliver beyond your expectations, I'd like you to help me find more passengers. Does that seem fair enough?"

Because you're using an analogy, they have to connect the dots. This is your plane. They are a passenger. *"My job is to get you from where you are to where you want to be safe and on time. As I deliver beyond your expectations, would you help me find more passengers?"*

When they say yes, you say:

"Well, the next time you're in a conversation with somebody and they mention they'd like to live in your neighborhood or even sell their home and move out of your neighborhood, would you take out your cell phone, look up my number and call me immediately?"

The analogy gives you a chance to embed that request right afterwards.

This is a really great dialogue to use on an initial consultation to plant the referral seed. You're using analogies. Analogies are easier ways to work with words to help people get an image of what you want, to go in the back door into their unconscious mind. It's like a little trap door back here.

The unconscious mind knows exactly what you're saying. It's easier for people to receive the request this way.

***Exact Ways to Ask 24* – 6 Spades**
To see the video training in the
Magic Words Dojo for this dialogue, go to:
www.byreferralonly.com/WayToAsk24
(you will need to be logged in)

Exact Way to Ask 25

The Easiest Way to Start a Casual Referral Conversation in Any Social Setting

Here's a way to generate an enormous stream of referral leads in any social setting. The dialogue goes like this:

"I was wondering if your best friend was going to buy, sell or borrow. Do you know an agent or a lender that you would feel comfortable introducing them to?"

What do you say if they say no?

"*I would love to be that person you feel comfortable introducing your friends to who need real estate or mortgage advice."* And then you can add a softener by saying, *"I'm wondering what would have to happen right now for us to make that a reality?"*

Now this is a great dialogue because it covertly asks, *"Do you have an agent or a lender that you trust for someone else?"* If they say no, it means they don't have one for themselves either because if they don't have one for a friend, they don't have one for themselves.

Now when you ask, *"What would have to happen to make that a reality?"* it generates a conversation. It's done gently. The embedded command is ***"right now for that to become a reality?"*** and that causes the mind to think about it.

The initial reaction will be "Not right now." Here's how to address that.

Learn how to talk about yourself in stories. So when you get into a referral conversation, you say:

"Well, what's happening in the market right now is there's a wonderful opportunity if somebody's living in an apartment. Let me just tell you recently what happened to a young couple who had a $2,000.00 a month rent payment and they wanted to live in a home, but keep their house payment equivalent to what they're paying in rent, and they needed some advice. So I was able to give them the advice, and today because of that advice, they now have a great three-bedroom, two-bath home. If you have a friend who needs that type of advice, maybe we can make that a reality and you could introduce them to me."

Now they're not going to say, *"Well, here is what we need to do."* They're going to say, *"Well, I don't know. Do you have a card?"*

When they say that, you say:

"Well yes, of course I have a card, but let me explain to you the different ways that I am helping people today, and I'll share with you briefly what happened with a person who was living over on Hiawatha and they had their home for sale for 16 months with a real estate agent, and they were introduced to me by a really good friend, and they wanted to sell that home and they just needed somebody who would give them the right advice. So I was able to come in and talk to them about adjusting their price and some other terms and as a result today, they got their home sold. So maybe you have a friend that has their home for sale right now that is not getting sold and they need that type of advice."

Are you following me on this? What you're doing when you say, *"What do we have to do right now to make that a reality?"* is you're opening up a conversation.

I would encourage you to use words like *"I'm wondering"* and *"I'm curious."* Those are called softeners and what they do is they prepare a person for a question.

"I'm curious, what would we have to do to make that a reality?"

Or "*I'm wondering what we would have to do right now to make that a reality?"*

It makes it a little easier for people to hear the question when you soften it a bit.

The Best Time to Use This Dialogue…

Imagine I'm at a cocktail party and somebody brings a friend over and says, *"Hey, Tom. This is Joe and Joe is my real estate agent."*

"Hey, Tom. Hey, Larry. Thanks for introducing us."

Larry says, *"Oh you're welcome."*

I say, *"Hey, Larry, isn't it nice to know that you have a friend in the real estate business that you feel comfortable referring your friend, Tom, to?"*

Larry chuckles, *"Yes. This guy is always promoting himself."*

I would turn to Tom and say, *"Hey, Tom. I'm curious, if your best friend right now needed to get real estate/mortgage advice, do you have an agent that you would feel comfortable introducing them to if they needed advice, just like Tom introduced me to you?"*

It's a nice way to open up for them to say, *"Well, yes, my brother's in the business."*

So you can say, *"Oh, that's excellent. Well, Tom and I have been working together and the best way to describe Tom is he is my ideal client."*

The secret is whenever you get an opportunity to ask somebody if they have a friend they would be comfortable referring their best friend to, **you're saying the word "friend" over and over again**.

Here is the entire dialogue all together.

I meet somebody and they say, "What do you do?"

"Well, thank you for asking. The best way to describe it is with a quick story. There's a young couple that lived in an apartment not far from here and they wanted to live in a home of their own and they needed some advice and they turned to get that advice and today as a result they are living in a beautiful three-bedroom home, two-baths over on Hiawatha Street and that's what I do is I make dreams come true for people who are looking for their first home."

They go, *"Oh, that's good. Well how do you that?"*

"Well, let me ask you if your best friend who was living in an apartment and they were thinking about moving into a home of their own, do you have a friend who is in the real estate business that you'd feel real comfortable recommending and referring them to that could help give them the advice they would need to move into a home of their own?"

"Oh no, I really don't know anybody."

"I'd love to be that person that you would feel comfortable recommending and introducing to people that you care about. I'd love to do that and I'm just curious, I mean right now, what would we have to do to make something like that happen?"

"No, no. I don't know anyone right now."

"Well, I really appreciate just having this conversation with you right now and thinking about that and now that we've talked about it, chances are real good that you're going to notice some of your closest friends and family members who are going to need my advice and would you be comfortable if I

just check back with you maybe 30 or 60 days from now and see if anyone comes to mind?"

"No, I wouldn't mind you doing that."

"Well the best thing I might be able to do for you now is do some research. Because I'd love to do some research for you and I could send you a monthly email. It tells you what all the homes are selling for in your neighborhood or how long they've been on the market, what the list price is, the sales price ratio and I know if you had that information, you could share it with your friends and you'd all feel secure in the knowledge of what's going on in your marketplace. I imagine that will be pretty valuable to you, would it not? Where would you like me to send that to?"

You're starting to weave it all together and that's what I want you to do—to be able to dance with all of the language. They're **like** arrows in a quiver and you can pull them out together or separately and use them.

So I could see you being in a social setting answering, *"How is the market?"* You have that casual conversation and somebody's saying, *"No, I don't know anyone."*

Then it's all woven together and the beauty is that you're keeping that conversation alive about them feeling good, then becoming aware, then noticing, then thinking about you and then introducing you to people.

It's a fabulous dialogue, a beautiful way to get into a casual referral conversation.

***Exact Ways to Ask 25* – 7 Spades**
To see the video training in the
Magic Words Dojo for this dialogue, go to:
www.byreferralonly.com/WayToAsk25
(you will need to be logged in)

Exact Way to Ask 26

Twenty-Four Words that Generated $4,500 in Commission in Less than 30 Seconds

The most important piece of this dialogue is in the little statement, *"Hey, what can we do right now to make sure that I get to speak to him, meet with him before he sells his home?"*

The script goes like this:

"Who's the next person you know that's most likely to buy, sell or borrow?"

The response is something like, *"That would be my father."*

"Well, what can we do together right now to make sure he has an opportunity to meet with me and speak with me before he sells his home? Because I'm sure you want to make sure he gets the best advice so this transition is easy and profitable for him, don't you?"

"Who is the next person?" actively assumes that everyone knows someone. **The secret is to ask in a tone of voice that assumes they know someone**.

It's so powerful when you say, *"Who is the next person that you know that's most likely to do what you just did?"*

There's a very active assumption. The word "next" causes the brain to go into search mode and actually look it up mentally and think, *"Who would be the next person?"* You can always tell if a person's actually looking it up, because their eyes will go up left.

So they're looking up to the left right now, thinking, *"Let's see, who could the next person be?"*

You know that they're searching and you use the words *"I'm curious"* or *"I'm just wondering, what can we do together right now?"*

"Is this the right time to ask for that to make sure that your dad has the opportunity to meet and speak and do that before he sells his home?"

Now, insert **because**. *"Because I'm sure you want to make sure that he gets the best advice."*

I like that because there. Used in this place it's very trance-like and the next thing you say has more power.

I like the word sell instead of list because list is our language. Sell is their language. So when people say *"I'm going to sell my home,"* they're really saying, *"I'm going to list it."*

What to Say When They Know another Agent/Lender

Everyone knows another real estate agent or another lender. I believe that is true in all market places, so it's really important that you understand the gap between *"Hey, my dad's thinking about moving"* and the person referred to.

It's a dangerous time right now because everyone knows another agent or lender and so how fast can you get to that introduction? The word "because" gives a reason to make the introduction.

I think of a time when Todd Welsh was sitting with his attorney, and his attorney said, *"Hey, my brother is going to be making a move and I told him to give you a call. Did you hear from him yet?"*

Todd said, *"I didn't hear from him. Do you want me to talk to him?"*

He goes, "*Yes, I want you to talk to him."*

Todd was about to leave, but then he remembered part of his dialog and he said to the attorney, *"Well I'm curious, what could we do right now to make sure that I get to meet him and speak to him before he sells his home? Because I know that you want him to get the best advice so he can have an easy, smooth, profitable transition. What can we do right now?"*

The guy literally picked up his phone, called his brother, and said, *"Hey brother, here's Todd. Talk to him."* He handed Todd the cell phone.

Todd reflected that back to me and said he would never have gotten that commission without that dialogue, because when he met with his attorney, the guy had two or three other people he knew in the business. But Todd was able to get the sale and make a $4,500.00 commission by knowing what to say in the moment.

How much does it cost you when somebody tells you, *"Yes, my dad's thinking about moving,"* and you say, *"Well, here's my business card. Would you have him give me a call?"*

Later you bump into your friend and say, *"Hey, what'd your dad do?"*

"Oh, he didn't call you? Well, anyway, he ended up listing his house with ABC and now he feels bad that you didn't get the referral and he doesn't refer anymore because he has this feeling that when he refers, he doesn't feel good."

You've got to be careful that if somebody introduces or identifies a referral, you've got to make the introduction happen, because that's what will make that person feel good.

I know I get discouraged when I refer my friends to an expert and my friends don't follow through. For example, I referred my sister Jeannie to a real estate agent up in the San Francisco area and she delayed on it. She didn't do anything, and she didn't do anything, and she didn't do anything.

I was disappointed because I wanted her to work with somebody who'd give her really great advice, somebody who would sit and counsel with her. She was buying her first place, but she delayed, and then she lost interest.

If I would've been conscious of this, I should have said, *"Jeannie, I'm going to make the connection for you. Let me get an agent on the phone, and I'll get the two of you together and I'll arrange for the introduction."*

But I lost the opportunity to refer her because I didn't follow through. I'm the one that didn't carry it through and I get discouraged when referring people if I don't have a mechanism to follow through and make the connection happen.

So imagine how your clients feel. If they have a sister, a brother, a cousin, an aunt, an uncle, a dear friend that's going to buy or sell and they want to refer you and they give their name to that person, but that person doesn't connect with you they get discouraged. They get frustrated at their friend. *"Why didn't you call?"*

It's our job to facilitate the introductions, our job to make it happen, and there's nothing better than getting a call from somebody who says, *"Hey, I just got done talking to my sister. She's waiting for a phone call from you. Would you call her right now? She wants to list her property."*

There's nothing better than that. Ever get a call like that? I mean *that's* an introduction. Or you get an email, *"Here is their name, their address, their phone number, their email address. We're expecting you right now."*

Nothing better than that!

***Exact Ways to Ask 26* – 8 Spades**
To see the video training in the
Magic Words Dojo for this dialogue, go to:
www.byreferralonly.com/WayToAsk26
(you will need to be logged in)

Exact Way to Ask 27

How to Make Sure People Don't Think You Are too Busy for Them

You need to make sure people understand you have time to help them.

Why?

Because if you don't they'll assume you don't have time for them!

The Magic Words go like this:

"I know that you're busy, so I'm going to keep this brief. I have time right now to help a few new clients who want to buy, sell or borrow in the next 30 to 90 days. I was going to place an ad in the paper asking 'Who do you know who wants to buy, sell or borrow in the next 30 to 90 days?' Then I thought, before I start dealing with people neither of us even know, I thought I'd give you a quick call and offer my time to the people who might need it. I'm curious, as you think about some of the people you know who could benefit from my help, who's the next person you know who would love to own their own home or is most likely to do what you just did?"

It's a very hypnotic suggestion when you say to people, *"I was going to place an ad in the paper asking..."* and then the quote... *"Who do you know who wants to buy, sell or borrow in the next 30 to 90 days?"*

Don't ask for their time...assume it!

Don't ask if they have time to talk. You're not calling them up to take time away from them. You're calling to give your time to them. You're saying, *"I've got time,"* and you just go right into it.

You dial and when they answer you say, *"Hey John, I know you're busy so I'm going to keep this brief."* Go right into it, and ignore the tendency to say, *"Hey, do you have a minute to talk?"*

If they answered the phone, assume they have time.

Also, you're offering time versus *need*.

"I have some time right now to help a few new clients and before I run an ad in the paper that says 'Who do you know who wants to buy, sell or borrow in the next 30 to 90 days?' I thought I'd call you."

It's as if you're saying, *"I don't need it; I just want to offer my time to you."*

Absent of them knowing that you have time, the automatic assumption is you're busy. Probably one of the healthier things you could do for your business at least once or twice a year is let people know that you have time for them, because if you go too long without contacting people the assumption is you're busy.

I can't tell you how many times people have said to me, *"Joe, I was going to get a hold of you, but I know how busy you are."*

They're saying that because I'm not actively calling them. I'm not pursuing them. So absent of me calling regularly, they think I'm really busy.

Does that make sense to you?

You've got to let them know that you have time for them.

What are the implications of people thinking you're too busy to help them?

They stop noticing other people, they stop thinking about you and they stop introducing you when you're too busy.

"Why would I even notice anyone who wants to buy, sell or borrow? You're just too busy. Why would I even think of you? You're too busy. Why would I introduce you? You're going to be too busy."

When people say, *"I know you're busy right now,"* what they're saying to you is, *"I know you don't have time."*

You've got to reframe that for them.

"Oh, it's important that you know that I do have time for you. I do have time for your friends and your neighbors. As a matter of fact, before I run an ad in the paper to attract somebody that neither of us know, I'll always call and ask you, 'Who do you know who's going to be buying, selling or borrowing in the next 30 to 90 days that I could invest my time with?"

I have a friend who belongs to a local church and he was sharing with me that there are two real estate agents in his church. One is a very experienced, very successful real estate agent. The other one is new and struggling to get going. A woman in the church was buying a house and chose to work with the very successful agent.

My friend asked her, *"Why did you choose the successful agent over the other agent?"*

She told him that she was always under the impression the new agent was too busy. Why? Because as a new agent, sometimes you get one deal going and you act like you're overwhelmed with all the transactional details. You give an impression to people that you don't have time, while the more successful agent who's got more business and whose time is much scarcer, is not projecting *"I don't have time."*

He's projecting, *"I'm here to help."*

You've got to be very conscious of putting on that busy-bee bonnet, where you run around saying, *"Oh, I'm doing great in my business, I'm so busy."* You're yelling *"I don't have time."*

It's a way of being.

You know people in your office who have that persona called *"I'm so busy,"* and they only have one transaction going. But they're sending a message that says, *"Don't notice, don't think of me, and don't introduce me to people because I just don't have time for them."*

That is the furthest thing from the truth, but absent of anything else, people are going to assume you're busy and that you don't have time for them if you don't let them know that you're available.

***Exact Ways to Ask 27* – 9 Spades**
To see the video training in the
Magic Words Dojo for this dialogue, go to:
www.byreferralonly.com/WayToAsk27
(you will need to be logged in)

Exact Way to Ask 28

Ask People for Their Advice and They'll Help You Get Business!

Imagine you're on the telephone during your hour of power and you're calling up a client who has referred someone to you in the past. You say:

"Hey Carl, this is Joe and there's two reasons I'm calling you today. One is I want to sincerely say thank you for trusting me to consult, negotiate, and oversee the transactional details for you when you sold your home and I'm truly grateful.

Now number two is to ask you for some advice. Imagine if you were me and you were a real estate consultant and you wanted to help more people who need real estate or mortgage advice and you only wanted to help the people you already know. I'm curious, what would you do to encourage others to introduce people to you?"

This is a great hour of power script for existing clients who have already referred someone to you. Asking people for advice is one of the highest compliments you can pay.

"Sure. What do you want, Joe?"

"Well, imagine if you were me and you were a real estate consultant and you wanted to do business with people who are like you and I'm wondering what would you do to encourage people who want to do business with you, that you'd want to introduce to them. What would you do?"

What you're sincerely asking for is: if they were in your position how would they go about doing it?

I've done this with a people who say things like, *"Well you know, you ought to come to our church on Sunday. I could introduce you to some people."* Or, *"We're doing a barbecue next weekend. You can stop by there. I could introduce you to some people."*

Sometimes people will say something like, *"Well, have you tried running an ad?"* They will start to give you advice on what they think is a good way for you to get business, which starts to open up a dialogue on how they can help you get business. Then they'll start to notice different ways they can help you and it opens up their reticular activator.

Many times people can help you if they put it into the form of telling you what they would do.

Some people don't have the capacity to help you unless they're telling you what to do. Maybe you've met people like that. They feel best when they're in instruction mode and they're telling you what to do, as opposed to doing it for you.

It's really simple. You're calling somebody who has already referred someone or who's already done business with you. They may have referred someone to you in the past or they may not have, but they've done business with you and you're thanking them.

"I'm really grateful for letting me consult and negotiate and oversee the transactional details for you and I'm really thankful and I need to get a little advice from you and that's what I'm going to ask for right now. Can you just give me a little bit of advice? If you were me and you were in the real estate and the mortgage business and you wanted to help more people who needed real estate or mortgage advice and you only want to help people you already know, I'm curious what would you do to encourage people who you already know to introduce you to the people that they know?"

Watch what happens. I think you'll be really pleasantly surprised.

***Exact Ways to Ask 28* – 10 Spades**
To see the video training in the
Magic Words Dojo for this dialogue, go to:
www.byreferralonly.com/WayToAsk28
(you will need to be logged in)

Exact Way to Ask 29

"Who's the NEXT Person You Know that Is Most Likely to Sell Their House?"

The intention with all these dialogues is to be able to move into a conversation naturally when you're at a cocktail party, a meeting, standing in line at Starbucks, at a conference, or wherever you are.

To do that, you need to understand the structure and how the dialogues work. Let's take this dialogue and look at its parts to see how we can piece it together and make it conversational.

The dialogue goes like this:

"Who is the ***next*** *person you know that is most likely to buy their first home? I know you know someone. As you continue scanning through the people you know who need my help, who comes to mind first?"*

After they answer you say, *"I'm curious. What do you think would be the best way to introduce us?"*

The secret word is "next" because "next" is the type of word that puts the mind into search mode.

If I were to say *"Who do you know that wants to buy a home?"* it would be like putting them in a corner, demanding they know somebody who's ready right now. But when I say *"Who's the* ***next*** *person you know?"* they have to start looking at people to see who's next.

When I learned this technique 15 years ago, I was practicing it with a woman named Pat Sherman. Pat was in Dayton, Ohio. We were with a group, sitting in a conference table in a hotel room. It was lunch time and waiters were coming in and out and I said to the group, *"You guys watch this."*

I turned to the waiter closest to us and asked, *"Do you know anyone who's going to buy a home maybe in the next six to eight months?"*

The waiter said, *"No, I don't know anybody."* It ended that fast.

After he left I asked the group, *"So what did you notice?"*

They all kind of came to same conclusion, *"Well, he just didn't know anybody."*

We then had a discussion about how it's not that he didn't know anyone, it was the way that I asked.

Whatever response I get is a result of what I've said. Everyone knows someone. If I have the mindset that everyone knows someone, I ask with that intention. It's how you ask that's going to give them the capacity to access who they know.

A bit later another waitress walks in. I said to the group, *"Now notice if you can spot the difference."*

The waitress was serving coffee and I said to her, *"You know, you're with a group of some of the best real estate agents and lenders here in the Dayton area. Pat Sherman and her team and her mortgage assistants are here and we're planning out what we're going to be doing for the next year. I'm curious. Who's the next person you know that's most likely to buy their first home here in the Dayton area?"*

It was amazing. We watched the waitress stop and her eyes looked up to the left. She was scanning her mind in that moment. She was looking and looking. When people look like that, it means they heard your request. If she would have said, *"Oh, I don't know anyone,"* I would believe she was so busy serving coffee that she didn't stop to hear the request.

When I say, "*Who's the next person you know?*" the word *next* is embedded. Whenever you're going to embed a command, you pause right before you embed it. You raise your voice slightly. You have a downswing. And then you pause.

So you'd say, *"Who is the* (pause, then emphasize with a falling voice) ***next, person you know*** (pause) *who's most likely to buy their first home in the Dayton area?"*

The waitress thought and then said, "*If it's going to be anybody, it'd probably be my dad.*"

When she left everyone around the table said, *"Can you believe that?"* as if it was some magic trick.

If you give people the right command, it goes into their unconscious mind and starts to do its work.

If I were with a senior citizen and their center of influence might be people who are in larger homes and now it's time for them to downsize into a smaller environment, I might say to them, "*Hey, who's the next person you know who's most likely to do what you just did? You moved into the senior citizen's facility and you had to sell your larger home. I know you know someone.*"

You're allowing them to access their resources to help you.

How to Decode Body Language to Know If They Are Comfortable Introducing Someone to You

Become aware of people's body language when you ask for an introduction. Become conscious of their level of comfort, because the biggest issue you're dealing with when you're asking people for an introduction is how they *feel* about giving an introduction.

What's the feeling that they have?

The number one reason people refer is because it makes them feel good.

I was at a Strategic Forum and Bill Anastasopolous walked up to me and said, *"Thank you so much for referring Garrett Gunderson's book* Killing Sacred Cows.*"*

Just for a second I felt so good that he had read the book and it inspired me. I thought, *"Oh man. I got a couple others, Bill, which you're going to really love to read too."*

So I refer because I like the way I feel when I get feedback from people who enjoyed the person that I referred.

Understand that when you're asking people for an introduction, referral or recommendation, they have a certain feeling about introducing.

It could be based on a past experience. It could be based on having been introduced in the past to something that didn't work out for them.

If they were introduced to a restaurant, movie, book, realtor or lender and it didn't work out, then they have this history of no longer receiving introductions from people. That's their internal language.

So when you're asking for an introduction you need to see how people are receiving what you're saying. You need to be noticing their level of comfort around it because that's going to take you in different directions.

When people say to you, *"Oh I really don't feel comfortable with that,"* you have a dialogue for helping people.

In this program, as we're coaching, I'm working with you to be able to weave and dance all these dialogues together. You're learning what to be listening for and how to be watching their body language, so you know what they're saying, not just with their words, but also with the way they're moving.

So if someone says, *"Oh no, no. I don't really know anyone,"* and they didn't look up left, then you know they didn't really look. So you might explore that.

If they say, *"No, I don't know anyone,"* you might help them explore that a little by saying, *"It feels a little bit to me that you may have had some bad experiences. Is that true? Is it possible you're saying that you may have had a bad experience referring people or introducing people?"*

Picture It *Before* You Do It

What I want you to do is just get a picture in your mind of the word 'introduce'. Just think of the different ways people can introduce.

For example I have this picture in my mind of a three-way phone call.

Somebody calls their person. They conference me in and they have this introduction occurring.

The person is saying, "Hey, Bob, this is Joe. He's on the other line. Joe, I want you to meet Larry."

I can see that in my mind. I can feel what it's like to be on the phone and that occurring.

I can also see in my mind an email being sent out. I can see a person writing an email and saying, *"Dear Tom, I want to introduce Joe to you and let me tell you a little bit about what Joe can do to help you."*

I can see that person clicking Send. I can see that as an introduction.

I can see a person physically introducing me, turning and saying, *"I want you to meet Joe Stumpf. He's a real estate agent. He's a mortgage consultant. I'd like you to meet him."*

I can see this happening at a party, in a social setting, at a restaurant. I can see the introduction occurring.

I can see a person writing a little handwritten note saying, *"Dan, I want you to meet my friend Joe. Enclosed is his business card. I really want to introduce him to you so you can meet him."* I can see that occurring, too.

Before I call, if I'm talking to Nancy and Nancy is referring me to Dan, I can see Nancy calling Dan and saying, *"Hey Dan, Joe is going to be calling you in 15 minutes."* I can see that as an introduction.

Get in your mind the idea of what it looks like when you're asking someone for an introduction. What are you actually asking them to do? Are you actually asking them to put a three-way call together? Are you actually asking them to provide an email for you? Do you actually want a letter for them? Do you want a note written? Do you want him do a pre-call for you? Or do you want him to orchestrate it in person?

What are you asking for?

If you know the outcome before you start talking, you're more likely to get it than if you're not sure of what you want the outcome to be.

If you're meeting with a current client and you know that the outcome you want for them is to introduce you to a person they mentioned during the transaction, and you want that introduction to happen now with a three-way call, it's more likely to happen.

By deciding the outcome in advance, you will start communicating in the direction of making that outcome come true.

It's really important no matter where you are, in any situation, when somebody says, "*Hey, a friend of mine is thinking about moving,*" the light bulb that you want to go on right away is:

"How do they get me introduced to them? What's the way that we get the connection to occur?"

Because you know that if you walk away without a connection, the likelihood of that person using your services significantly drops—because everybody knows another realtor. Everybody knows another lender.

***Exact Ways to Ask 29* – J Spades**
To see the video training in the
Magic Words Dojo for this dialogue, go to:
www.byreferralonly.com/WayToAsk29
(you will need to be logged in)

Exact Way to Ask 30

How to Turn Every Compliment into a Chance for a Referral

When somebody says something positive to you, they say, *"Hey, thank you. You've done a great job for us."* You say:

"Well, my pleasure, John. You'd do the same for me. You can always count on me and I know that I can always count on you to introduce me to the people that you care about because you want your family, your friends and neighbors to get the best advice when it's time to buy, sell or borrow, don't you? I mean I'm curious. Who is the next person you know that is most likely to buy, sell or borrow?"

The law of reciprocity is being used here. **When someone says something positive, others want to do the same in return.**

So when they say, *"Hey, thank you very much,"* they're acknowledging they received something from you. They're giving you a compliment and one way to receive that is by giving them permission to get even with you.

So when somebody says, *"Hey, thanks for doing a real nice job for you,"* you now have a chance to let them even the score. That's what most people want.

It's been proven in all types of studies that when somebody receives something, there's a chemical reaction that says, *"I want to give you something in return."*

We want to give back when we receive something.

For years adherents of the *Hare Krishna* sect would walk up to you at the airport and pin a flower on you and wait for you to give them a donation in return, because there's an automatic chemical reaction that says, *"I want to give you something for that."*

That's why you almost say, *"No. Don't do that,"* because you know it's going to cost you in terms of reciprocity.

One day I'm sitting in the airport and a guy walks up to me and hands me a pencil with a little note. Then he walks away and the pencil says, *"I'm deaf. If you'd like to keep this pencil, please make a donation."*

He knows that the longer I hold the pencil, the more likely I'll give a donation. If he walks up to me and says, *"Would you like to give me a donation,"* he's asking before he's giving. If he gives me the pencil first, it's mine. Now I want to give him something in return.

It's the law of reciprocity and it's very, very powerful.

When we get something, there's a part of us that thinks it's natural to want to give back. So allow that to happen. Make that happen.

When you say, *"You know, you can always count on me to deliver exactly what I say I'm going to do and I know I can count on you to introduce me to the people that you care about,"* you're just affirming that you are the same.

It's like you want them to be looking at a mirror. They see themselves. The words *my pleasure* are a wonderful phrase. When somebody gives you any type of acknowledgement you can say, *"My pleasure."*

Another nice phrase is, *"Thank you for noticing. Thank you for saying something."*

"My pleasure. As a matter of fact, you know that you can count on me and I know that I can count on you."

You are stating it as something that is very, very certain.

Why You Should Ask for a Referral When People Are Feeling Gratitude

During the transaction, there are lower frequencies called fear, worry and anxiety. Then there are higher frequencies called gratitude, thankful, happy and delighted.

The middle range is being satisfied, encouraged or okay. *"We're feeling copasetic. Everything's okay."*

So when you're doing your hour of power and you say to people, *"Hey, how are you guys feeling?"* They go, *"We're doing okay."* This is not the appropriate time to even talk about an introduction or a referral.

The referral moment is when people give a high frequency answer, *"Hey, we're doing great. We're really thankful for everything you've done."*

When people say, *"You know, we're a little bit worried right now,"* your job is to see if you can get them past satisfied. Can you get them up to **delighted**?

"Okay. Before I hang up, I want to ask them how they're feeling. I'm looking for gratitude. When I get gratitude, then I can ask."

The worst time to ever ask is when people are in fear. When they say, *"Well, we're a little concerned, Joe. This thing is going to close on Tuesday,"* you can't say:

"Well, I'm a little worried, too. But do you know anyone else who'd like to go through this with me?"

It's really inappropriate the way some people ask for a referral. They just don't have any sense of timing at all.

You should always ask when someone gives you a good solid compliment. It's like aikido. It's turning the compliment into a referral.

Exact Ways to Ask 30 **– Q Spades**
To see the video training in the
Magic Words Dojo for this dialogue, go to:
www.byreferralonly.com/WayToAsk30
(you will need to be logged in)

Exact Way to Ask 31

How to Finally Deal with People Who Don't Refer!

About 15% of the population simply won't advocate for anyone.

When they say, *"I just don't know anyone,"* you might want to check to see if they're part of the 15% or if it's simply that right now, they just don't know anyone.

Here's a dialogue on how to handle referral rejection:

"Well, that's fine. I'm curious to know if that's because you aren't entirely comfortable discussing introductions in general or simply because no one's come to mind ***yet****..."*

The Magic Word is "yet"*...*

"Or is there something that would have to happen for you to get to the point where you feel entirely comfortable introducing me to someone who would benefit from my help?"

It's a great dialogue just to open up a conversation. Now if a person says, *"No, I just don't know anyone and I'm not going to refer you anyone,"* they could be part of that 15% of the population that just doesn't introduce or recommend anyone.

When people fall into that category, more than likely they've had a bad experience and they don't feel good about it. That's what I've heard from people who just don't refer anymore. They just had a bad experience and once you have a bad experience recommending somebody, particularly in real estate or in mortgage banking, it's hard to do it again.

Remember, the number one reason people refer is to make themselves feel good. If they refer somebody and it made them feel bad, they don't want to do it again because they don't want to feel bad again.

Another reason is that there might be something missing in the equation. When you're asking for a referral, maybe you're not asking in a way that is connecting with them. Maybe there's something missing from your request. So this dialogue is used only after you've asked a couple of times with people.

Suppose you've asked this person three or four times over the course of four or five years and they've never referred anyone to you. During your next hour of power, you might want to see what's really going on there, see what the truth is.

Suppose you're evidencing success, sending letters from the heart, inviting them to client events, and it's now your Hour of Power. This is the fifth phone call over the course of three years. They've never introduced anyone even in the "during" unit. You might want to just see what's going on there.

What's missing right now? Are they part of the 15%? Did they have a bad experience? What's missing?

***Exact Ways to Ask 31* – 2 Clubs**
To see the video training in the
Magic Words Dojo for this dialogue, go to:
www.byreferralonly.com/WayToAsk31
(you will need to be logged in)

Exact Way to Ask 32

How to Handle "I Just Don't Know Anyone That I Can Refer to You"

Here's a very simple and elegant way to handle any type of resistance:

They say, *"I just don't know anyone that I can refer to you who is buying right now."*

"Well, thank you for taking the time to even think about it and I understand how you feel. a good friend of mine, Larry Anderson, felt the same way when I asked him to introduce me to the people he cared about, but he found..."

Notice how the "but" erases everything before...

"...but he found that a few days after we spoke, he started noticing friends who were talking about buying a larger, more spacious home and I'm wondering would you be comfortable if I check back with you in 30 days to see if you found anyone."

That extra little "found" at the end is neat to play off of. It is part of the concept of the concept: "Feel, Felt, Found."

So when somebody says they want to price their home at $325,000 and you know in your mind that the home is worth $310,000, you can deal with it using Feel, Felt, Found:

"I know how you ***feel****. a friend of mine or a client of mine, John,* ***felt*** *the very same way and after I showed him what homes were selling for he* ***found*** *it would be better off if he put the home on market for $350,000.00* ***because*** *it would help him get his five, six and seven."*

What you do is you just insert a story wrapped around Feel, Felt Found.

There's complete agreement that what they're saying is valid, *"I know how you feel."* You really have to say it like you know how they feel. So when someone says, *"I really want more money for my house,"* you say:

"Well, I really do know how you ***feel*** *and the reason I know is I have a client who I work very closely with for a number of years who* ***felt*** *the very same way and I sat down, I showed him what homes were selling for in his area, then we compared it to what was important to him based on what his timeline was to get home sold, and he* ***found*** *that he was better off putting it on the market for $310,000 and we were able to* ***get that home sold*** *in 62 days, and he was able to* ***move on with life****. So I'm going to suggest that you do the very same thing that I suggested to my friend, and you'll find that we'll be able to help you* ***get your home sold*** *and you can* ***move on with life*** *when we price your home at $310,000."*

You're giving a reason why you believe that what you're suggesting is better than what they're suggesting based on a formula:

"I know how you ***feel****. Others have* ***felt*** *the same, and as a result of what they now know, here's what they* ***found****."*

It's next to magical when you insert it into a story.

Exact Ways to Ask 32 **– 4 Clubs**
To see the video training in the
Magic Words Dojo for this dialogue, go to:
www.byreferralonly.com/WayToAsk32
(you will need to be logged in)

Exact Way to Ask 33

How to Make Them Feel Good about Introducing You without Being Pushy

When you ask someone what it was like to refer other services to the people that they care about, you create a good feeling for them. You help them access the good feeling they have about referring.

Remember the reason people refer is for the feeling they get when they refer.

So the Magic Words would be:

"In the past, what's it been like when you introduced people to products and services that you really liked, and the people you introduced had a really positive experience with?"

Listen to their answers. Then say, *"Well, think of how good you'll feel knowing that you've made a positive difference in the lives of your friends and your family by telling them about me. I'm not going to say, 'Introduce me to the people you care about,' because only you know the people who are in the best position to benefit from my help. Isn't that right?"*

There are a lot of little things that are going on in this dialogue I would love you to be able to integrate into all of your language.

The first is the use of a negation and a quote at the same time, which you can use to say the "unsayable." "Now I'm not going to say…" allows you to quote yourself like:

"I'm not going to say 'I am the perfect agent to make your dream come true,' because that would be arrogant."

That allows you to say the unsayable.

You can say, *"I'm not going to say 'you're in safe hands with me' because that sounds like a cliché."*

"I'm not going to say, 'Sign the listing agreement right now,' because you may still have more questions that you want answered before you sign it."

"I'm not going to say, 'Buy this house,' because after looking at 81 homes in your price range, you'll have to decide if this is the one to buy."

How to Hook Them with a Past Experience

When you ask *"Can you remember a time?"* you're doing a thing called timeline therapy.

Imagine that our brains are set up with a horizontal line and each memory is installed on that line in its place. We've kind of integrated it into our cultural language when we say things like, *"Hey, I'm looking forward to seeing you next Tuesday."* What does that mean, looking forward? It means I'm going in my mind to a place in the future on my timeline and I'm placing you there. Or we say, *"Oh, I remember back in the 60's,"* meaning we go back on the timeline to the 1960's in our minds.

So when I'm saying to a person, *"What was it like when you introduced people to the products and services that you really liked and they had a really positive experience?"* I'm not simply saying:

"Remember when you referred somebody in the past?"

I have to add to it:

"...and they had a really positive experience."

Because if you just say, *"Remember referring somebody in the past?"* there's a tendency to go to the darkest memory first, because that's the one that has the most charge on it.

Our memories are installed in our brain according to the electrical charge that they have. The traumas, those things that we received with the most electrical charge to them, get stuck on the timeline.

You remember things that happened seven or eight years ago like it was yesterday, but you can't remember what you had for dinner last night because there's no charge on that memory.

I said to my daughter Traci, *"Do you remember what happened the day that I came in and I told you mom and I were going to separate?"*

She goes, *"I remember it clearly, Dad. We were in the living room, I was sitting on that orange sofa and..."*

She has this whole picture because she received that information with electrical trauma attached to it. But she can't remember her client's name that she cut hair on Tuesday morning. It's not as charged. Does that make sense?

When you say, *"Can you remember a time when you referred someone to a product or service?"* their instinct is to go back to the memory that has the most charge. So you have to add: *"And they really enjoyed the experience."* Then give them time to look for it.

It might be an event they have forgotten, so you may have to give suggestions.

"Have you ever recommended a restaurant? Have you ever recommended a book? Have you ever recommended a movie?"

You want them to associate with a feeling right now. *"Oh yeah, I remember that. Yeah, I've referred somebody to a great movie and they loved it."* Now you're connecting the feeling of introducing in the past with what's going to be occurring in the future.

Can you remember a time when you referred someone to By Referral Only, maybe to an event, and they had a great experience?

Maybe you can remember referring someone who didn't have a great experience, but can you remember somebody having a great experience? Or somebody that really enjoyed the seminar? Somebody who enjoyed a conference call or somebody who enjoyed a home study CD?

Do you remember that in the past?

So now you look. You're searching. Your brain is scanning and looking for that experience. It's going back along the timeline.

All you're doing is asking people to access old records and attach a feeling to it. Then you say, *"Well, think of how good you'll feel knowing that you've made a positive difference in the lives of your friends and your family by telling them about me."*

That's a very powerful statement to associate their past good feelings with you.

Think about the great, positive impact that you're going to have on family and friends and neighbors and people that you really care about when you tell them about me.

You guys are going to get so good at this. You're going to say to your kids, *"I'm not going to say make your bed because you know that's what you're supposed to do."*

"I'm not going to say get down here and have dinner right now, because you know that's what we're supposed to do at this time."

"I'm not going to say get down here right away because you know that's what you're supposed to do."

You've put the negation in front of the command.

"I'm not going to say introduce me to the people that you care about because only you know the people who are in the best position to benefit from my help. Isn't that true?"

So very powerful.

How good can they feel?

***Exact Ways to Ask 33* – 6 Clubs**
To see the video training in the
Magic Words Dojo for this dialogue, go to:
www.byreferralonly.com/WayToAsk33
(you will need to be logged in)

Exact Way to Ask 34

How to Talk to Their Unconscious Concerns

It's a fact that people have unconscious concerns about referring or introducing you and one of the biggest concerns is confidentiality.

That's why it's important you tell your clients how you will respect the relationship.

When you are working with close friends and family members, there is a boundary that you want to be careful that you don't cross.

This dialogue will usually come in handy when people are stalling.

I was talking to a young lady the other day who said her sister was working with another agent. She comes from a large family and she was asking me, *"What do you think the reason is that my sister is working with another agent?"*

I said, *"It's probably an unconscious concern and it might be something like confidentiality that you might discuss the finances with the rest of the family because you might do that type of stuff unconsciously right now, and she thinks if you do it with other people in the family, you might do it with her. It might be unconscious concerns that people have."*

So to address that concern, you would say:

"You know, you're probably already aware that when you introduce me to a friend, a family member or a neighbor, I'll always respect the confidentiality of the relationship and I vow never to share anything about your private business with them. I know this is important to you and I imagine knowing this will make it even easier for you to introduce me to some of the people you care about who might need my help."

When you choose to talk about other people when they're not present, like talking about other clients in front of your current client, unconsciously you're saying, *"I'm going to be talking about you in front of other people."*

I had a young man help me sell a house a number of years ago who was referred to us. It was when I was going through a marital breakup and he was referred to us by the court. He spent a lot of time talking to us about other people and in the back of my mind I'm thinking, *"Oh boy, this guy is going to be chitchatting about me because of who I was and I know that's going to happen."*

And sure enough, he had all of this little chitchat about me and my private life, and he was doing it in order to get in favor with another person. I just felt that feeling of "urgh!"

I heard it once said that there are three types of people. There are small thinkers—people whose conversation is usually about other people.

There are mediocre thinkers—people who talk about events.

There are big thinkers—people who talk about big ideas.

So when you're talking with somebody, are you talking with them about the big idea of getting their home sold? Are you talking about the events in your life? Or are you talking about other people?

When you talk about other people it unconsciously says to people, *"I might not be able to be trusted."*

Remember, the job of the unconscious mind is to eliminate the unknown, so that it can be comfortable, safe, and knowing.

If someone is wondering, *"Are you going to be talking about me to other people?"* they are in the unknown.

They're wondering, *"Is this going to happen when you leave here?"*

I started to think about all the other unconscious concerns people may have and I made a list of 7 unconscious concerns you may want to learn how to address by talking about them.

Unconscious concern 1:

People may think they've made bad decisions in the past when they picked someone without the advice or the input of other people. So when somebody says to you, *"I really want my brother to look at the house before I buy it,"* what they might be saying unconsciously is, *"In the past, I've made some bad decisions and I'm not so certain that without someone else's input that I won't make another bad decision."*

That might be the real unconscious concern. It might not be about the brother's opinion. It might be about them not wanting to be embarrassed.

Unconscious concern 2:

Another unconscious concern is they may not want to make a decision because they **don't want to be ridiculed** by other people for the decision they have made. They don't want to be judged by other people.

For example if they say, *"I need my mom to look at the house before I make a decision,"* it may not that they need their mom to see the house as if they're going to discuss the merits of the house with her. What's happening is they're unconsciously concerned that if they went ahead without their mom's approval, they'd have years of ridicule or guilt to suffer from if mom is the type that needs to be included in all her kid's decisions. So when people say something like that, you might want to just talk about it.

"Is it that you want your mom to look at the house because you need her opinion on it or is it because you want

your mom's approval on the decision?" and once you talk about it, usually disappears.

Unconscious concern 3:

Another unconscious concern is **they have fear**. When anybody goes into fear, they bring up their defenses and a big defense that people have is called *isolation*. Withdrawal, not returning phone calls, pulling back, cancelling appointments—those are not necessarily indications that they're not interested in buying or selling or getting a loan. They might just be in fear right now. And they might not even be aware they're in fear. So when somebody doesn't return your phone calls, say to them on your message, *"Hey, you're supposed to call me back today."* Then address the call:

"Hey, John. I imagine right now there might be a little bit of fear that you're going through because when you don't return my phone call, there might be something behind that behavior that says you might be afraid and that might or may not be true, but if you want to talk about any of your fears, please feel free to give me a call. I'd love to talk to you about it." That might be more the truth than what you're making up in your mind: *"They don't like me. I did something wrong."* You think it's about you, but it's really about their fear.

Unconscious concern 4:

Another unconscious concern is when you lack rapport and **they don't feel like you're an expert**. As soon as a person has the thought that you really don't know what you're talking about, that becomes an unconscious concern. You'll notice that people start to back off and you may want to address that, *"Is there something that's saying to you that you might believe I'm not the right person to handle this transaction for you?"*

Unconscious concern 5:

They **can't defend their decision** to refer you. That's an important thought because when people want to introduce you to the people they care about, they have to be able to defend their opinion. They have to be able to take a stand and almost represent you by saying, *"Okay, let me tell you why you should use him or her."*

Now I know that when somebody says to me, *"Well, I already know somebody in the business,"* if I don't have a good argument for it they might not even recommend you. So that might be an unconscious concern they'll have to defend against and they're not sure how.

Unconscious concern 6:

Another unconscious concern is **there's nothing really worth talking about you**. There's nothing really remarkable about you. I love that word *remarkable*. Seth Godin—if you go to www.sethgodin.com, you'll find the best blog in the world for marketing insight—talks about the word *remarkable*. Remarkable means: in such an exceptional experience that people go out and remark about it. They make mention of it. It's remarkable.

Some people might not remark about you because unconsciously there's nothing exceptional about you, and you may be thinking, *"Boy, they don't like me."* It might not be you. It might be their experience that they've had with you or they lack the education about what makes you different and remarkable.

If somebody says, *"Well, I already know someone in the business,"* they don't have a way to say, *"Well let me tell you about this remarkable person and what makes this person different."*

And if they don't have that, they might not introduce you because they don't want to feel like they don't know you well enough to talk about you.

Unconscious concern 7:

Another unconscious concern might be when your clients say to you, *"I really don't know anyone right now,"* but unconsciously what they're saying is, ***"I don't want you to get too busy that you won't have time for me."*** That's an unconscious thing.

Larry Siebert deals with that well. He tells people, *"I always have enough space in my life to work with 12 people at one time. Right now, I'm working with six so I have space and time to make sure to give you all the attention you need and still have room for six more people."*

He says that and keeps that commitment. He never works more than 12.

Those are a few of the things that you want to learn how to talk about so that it becomes easier for people to introduce you to the people they care about.

If they aren't referring you it may be because they saying things that aren't true, but are in their unconscious. They may not even be clear what's true, because it's hidden. It's buried underneath.

***Exact Ways to Ask 34* – 8 Clubs**
To see the video training in the
Magic Words Dojo for this dialogue, go to:
www.byreferralonly.com/WayToAsk34
(you will need to be logged in)

Exact Way to Ask 35

Everyone You Know Knows Someone Who Needs a Great Agent or Lender

Simply assume everyone knows someone who needs an agent or lender. I'll teach you why in just a minute.

Here's some great language. I want you to notice all the statements that have active assumption in them, and then I'll point them out after you're done reading it. See if you can find them on your own.

"I don't know if you've already begun to notice friends, family members and neighbors who can benefit from knowing about my consulting, negotiating and organizational skills. the next time you're in a conversation with a friend, family member or a neighbor and they mention that they would like to buy, sell or borrow, I know you wouldn't want them to miss out on the kind of benefits I've helped you get, so I'm wondering, how quickly can you pick up your cell phone and call me so that I can start helping right away?"

I love the thought that "Everyone Knows Someone."

Imagine there are three letters stamped on everyone's forehead: **E K S**.

Everyone Knows Someone.

It's a belief you start with, no matter what. Everyone knows someone.

They may not remember their name right now, but everyone knows someone and that empowers you when it's time to ask if you assume everyone knows someone.

Now, what are some of the statements that make assumptions? Look at this statement:

"I don't know if you've already begun to notice." There's a negation in front of it. *"I don't know if"* is the negation and the embedded command is, *"you've already begun to notice."*

It would be different if I just said, *"You've already begun to notice"* without using the negation first. You would say, *"No, I haven't."*

But when I say, ***"I don't know if*** *you've already begun to notice,"* there's more of an assumption than a command, because you put the negation in front of it.

"I don't know if you want to sign the contract right now or if you want to get more of your questions answered first."

"I don't know if you want to go ahead and buy this house or did you want to look at the agreement a little closer?"

When I'm using a negation, I can put the command in without being so direct. So when I say, *"I don't know if you want to go ahead and sign the listing agreement right now,"* the embedded command is ***"sign the listing agreement right now."***

When I put the words, *"I don't know if you want to,"* it allows me to give the suggestion of what I want them to do.

So when I say, *"I don't know if you've already begun to notice..."* the mind goes, *"I'm going to start noticing. Noticing what?"*

"Noticing friends, family members and neighbors who can benefit from knowing about my consulting, negotiating and overseeing the transactional detail skills."

Another very active assumption in the dialogue is "the next time."

"The next time you're in a conversation with someone and they mention..."

You're suggesting they're going to be in a conversation with someone. You're not saying *"If you're in a conversation with somebody,"* because that's not assuming they will.

But when you say, *"Hey, **the next time** you're in a conversation,"* it means they have to assume they're going to be in that conversation.

The next active assumption is, *"I know you wouldn't want them to miss out on the kind of benefits that I've helped you get. I know you wouldn't want to do that."*

"I know you wouldn't want your friends to work with an agent or a lender who wouldn't give them the advice that would help them get the best buy."

That is a very active assumption.

How Quickly Can You?

Using "How quickly can you?" is a bit of a pattern interrupt.

When I say, *"How quickly can you?"* I'm assuming they will call. I'm not saying *"Will you call?"* I'm saying, *"How quickly will you call?"* which is assuming they're going to call.

I love that. *"How quickly can you get your cell phone out, look up my number and call me? How quickly can you do that?"*

You're not saying *"Would you?"* You're saying *"How quickly would you?"* and that's actively assuming.

The last one is *"Start helping right away."* You're assuming that you're going to start helping them right away.

So you would say, *"I'm wondering, how quickly can you pick up your cell phone and call me so I can* ***start helping right away****?"*

I've noticed the successful people in business assume the role of success. They act as if they've already got the business. They're not asking for it; they're assuming they already have it. They completely assume the sale.

The moment they sit down, they're not asking, *"Will you list with me?"* They're saying, *"Once we get the home on the market, you're going to notice in the weeks, the days and the months ahead that you're going to be absolutely delighted that I'm the person who's overseeing your transactional details."*

When you are already assuming they've made that choice, you're putting yourself into the position of authority. They don't even have to decide; you've already made the decision for them.

I'm assuming that we're going to do this. That's a very powerful place, because as Emerson put it, "the mass of men are silently begging to be led."

People are unconsciously thinking, *"Don't make me appoint you, because then I have to decide and I don't want to decide. I want you to decide for me."*

It gives you a tremendous power. Take it upon yourself to assume that role.

When I say, *"I don't know if you've already begun to notice,"* you start to check out in your mind. *"Have I begun to notice? Have I not begun to notice?"*

Whatever follows goes into the unconscious mind. *"I don't know if you've already begun to* ***notice that this may be the perfect time to sign a listing agreement****."*

"I don't know if you've begun to notice that when you introduce me to your friends and your family members, that they're going to get some great consulting, negotiating, overseeing the transactional details when you introduce me to your friends or family members."

"I don't know if you've already begun to notice..."

Whatever you say next gets embedded there.

*"I don't know if you've already begun to notice where you may place some of your furniture as you **imagine yourself moving in**."*

*"I don't know if you've already begun to notice the feeling you experienced of selling your home as you **signed the listing agreement**."*

"I don't know if you've already begun to notice how much confidence you will feel with this dialog as you imagine the many conversations you will use it to help the people forward and towards their goals."

"I don't know if you've already begun to notice that the most successful agents and lenders assume the outcome they want and are more surprised that it doesn't occur when it does happen."

The secret is to be really surprised if you *don't* get the listing, versus being surprised when you do. The most successful lenders and agents think: *"I can't imagine what happened. I didn't get it?"* as opposed to *"Whoa, I got it!"*

So you're embedding that everyone's going to work with you.

I assume that you're going to become very good with this. I assume that you're going to read this over and over again. I just actively assume that and your behavior will usually follow what I assume you're going to do.

***Exact Ways to Ask 35* – 9 Clubs**

To see the video training in the
Magic Words Dojo for this dialogue, go to:
www.byreferralonly.com/WayToAsk35
(you will need to be logged in)

Exact Way to Ask 36

Help People Discover Places Where They Can Find People Who Need Your Help

Read this script a few times.

"The next time you're in a conversation with a friend from work or church or your golfing community or with a family member or with a friend and they mention that they are interested in…"

Here's where you get very specific…

"…interested in moving into a larger more spacious home / moving out of their condominium and owning a home of their own / resetting their loan so it can be more affordable, please don't keep me a secret."

Now the change I'm making on this card is whenever you use the words "please don't keep me a secret" you must follow it with the word "because."

You'd say, *"Because you feel so good when they thank you for introducing me to them so I can help them."*

I'll just emphasize this point: When you end your thought with the words *"please don't keep me a secret"* the unconscious mind only hears and remembers "keep me a secret" because *don't* is a negation. Whatever comes after the negation becomes the command.

When you use, *"Please don't keep me a secret,"* it's a pattern interrupt and you must follow it up with *"because…"* and then give your reason behind it:

"Because you will feel so good when they thank you for introducing me to them so I can help them."

Here it is again.

"Hey, next time you're in a conversation with a friend from work, from church, from your country club, from your bowling league, from the rotary club, from your BNI group and they mention that they're interested in moving into a larger home, maybe going from 2,500 square foot home, maybe up to 3,500 to 4,000 square foot home, please don't keep me a secret because you'll feel so good when they thank you for introducing me to them so I can help them."

Earlier we talked about how important the word "because" is, because everything that comes after it is strengthened by three times. You don't even have to give a real big reason. You can just say, *"Please don't keep me a secret because you want your friends to feel good."* Anything after the word *because* strengthens everything before it.

Help Them Think of Groups

It's important that you think of groups where people can notice people. Here are some powerful suggestions for doing that.

I wrote a program about seven years ago called the DIR program: the direct and indirect referral program. What I suggested in the program was that when you're on a listing appointment, set a goal to walk out of the house with 20 names, addresses, and phone numbers of the people in their centers of influence.

The easiest way to get the list is to *suggest to the client that there's a lot of people who may know someone who may know someone who may know someone who may know someone that would be interested in the home—and the easiest way to connect with those people would be that they would give you a list of 20 people they know and you'll send a flyer, a feature sheet or send an email to them talking all about your home or a virtual tour that they could forward to people that they know.*

AT&T did it many years ago, called the friends and family program, and they expanded business very rapidly using this tool.

So, when you're listing a property think of a wedding. If these people were going to get married, the average size wedding today is about 250 people. So, who would they invite? That becomes a big sphere of influence.

As you're talking to them, you're saying, *"When you talk about introducing me to the people that you care about, you'll have the inner circle which is about eight or nine people, their friends, their closest family members, and another ring around work associates, then another ring around that which starts going out to their dentist, their chiropractors and the family members of some of those associates that they have and it's kind of like you can spin out to the furthest edges."*

Then you give an example:

"*Ken and Marlene who live down the street from me—they would be on the furthest edge of my center of influence. At the closest ring inside would be my brother Johnny and my sister Marsha. And another ring out would be Jesse and another ring out would be some of the people at our office.*"

Every ring moves a little further away from the people they're capable of influencing. The people furthest out are the hardest to influence. The people closest in are easiest to influence.

So, when you think of groups that you want people to notice, start to think of all of their work associates, anyone that they would go out for dinner with. Think of their phone directory.

Actually I've often thought of saying it this way:

"Hey, when anybody in your telephone directory needs advice, any one that you know well enough that you put in to your cell phone directory, those are the people that you can

feel comfortable referring me to or introducing me to if they need advice or they need council."

So think in terms of those groups of people.

How to Get Them to Think Seasonally

What I mean by *seasonally* is the different times of the year when people move into motion.

So around the first of the year there are thoughts like, "Hey, I'm setting a New Year's resolution. I'm going to own a new home. We're going to buy a bigger home. We're moving out of an apartment. We're moving to a home of our own."

Around February there's Valentine's Day. It's the time when people get engaged, so you can start to say to people:

"Do you know anyone who's getting engaged?" You can also say that in March, because the possibility of them noticing it starts to become much higher then.

In June and July you can say, *"Anybody getting married? Are there any weddings you're going to?"* If anyone's going to a baby shower, it also means it's time that people may be in motion.

Bill Good says that people in motion have a tendency to stay in motion. So when somebody's pregnant they're beginning the motion of moving towards a bigger house. So, you might say:

"If you notice somebody's who's pregnant, think to yourself, 'Are they going to be needing a bigger home?' Then think of me, take your cell phone out, look up my number, and give me a call immediately." You're giving them a specific thing to look at.

The same goes for anything else you want them to notice, like if they have friends with college students who are moving out. You'd want to bring that up around September when kids are going back to school.

I was with a friend at diner and he said to me, *"Joe. You know, I was going to retire in six months, but I've decided I'm retiring in three weeks."* Everyone at dinner applauded.

I said, *"What are you going to do, Art?"*

"I'm selling my house and I'm moving to Florida."

He's going to go down to the Keys and he was like right there, ready to do it. I noticed and in that moment, I referred Art to a couple of the guys that I work with locally.

There's some really cool statistics that you can look up that show a good 60% of the people who clean their carpets are three months away from selling their house.

You can see that when people buy a brand new car, they're beginning the motion. New money came in to their life.

Car...house...that's the cycle.

I remember doing some work with Countrywide. Bob Lee told me a good 35% of all the people who were applying for a first mortgage had a new car on their credit report that showed up in the last six months.

It shows that when people start to go into motion, the motion continues towards improvement. You can start to notice when things are in motion and that's a signal that you can help.

By suggesting that people look at these groups, you're helping them to help.

"Hey the next time you're in a conversation with somebody who's pregnant and they may be considering a bigger home..."

"The next time you're in a conversation with somebody whose kids are going off to college…"

"Next time you're in a conversation with somebody at a baby shower…"

"Next time you're in a conversation with somebody who's going through a divorce…"

"Next time you're in a conversation with somebody who sets some really strong New Year resolutions to own a home of their own…"

When you give those types of suggestions, you're giving people permission to become aware. I could say to you:

"Hey, the next time a brand new agent comes into your office, they're right out of licensing school, they're just getting started and maybe the manager introduces them at your office, meaning to say this person's brand new, think of me. Take out your cell phone, look up our number and let us know how we can help them and even you could give them a CD, an 87-minute CD that could explain to him how they can set up a before, during and after unit."

I just embedded that thought for you, but it's very specific.

The next time you're in a meeting and somebody stands up and says, *"I'm new to the business"…*

What could you do next?

***Exact Ways to Ask 36* – K Clubs**
To see the video training in the
Magic Words Dojo for this dialogue, go to:
www.byreferralonly.com/WayToAsk36
(you will need to be logged in)

Exact Way to Ask 37:

How to Become Highly Skilled During Moments of Awkward Silence

When you embrace this whole philosophy around asking for introductions and referrals, you're going to come into situations where eventually somebody's going to just go silent when you ask.

You'll be asking, *"Who's the next person you know who'd like to buy a larger, more spacious home?"*

"Who's the next person you know that is going to be resetting their loan and they may need my help?"

Then there's going to be a pregnant pause.

Your beliefs are all going to come to the surface in that moment.

It's important that you have a dialogue you can access in that moment. The language would sound like this:

"Eventually, when you do come across a person who you think I could help, keep in mind that I'm never too busy to help your friends, family members and neighbors in the same way I've been able to help you.

So the next time you're in a conversation and a person mentions that they would like to buy a larger, more spacious home or mentions that their loan is being reset and they have to secure new financing, I'd like you to please call me immediately. So what happens Casey, when you imagine yourself doing that?"

I want to call your attention to the word "eventually" and I would encourage you to underline that word mentally or physically.

"Eventually" is such a nonspecific word that you can imagine almost anything happening *eventually*.

"Eventually, you're going to buy a home."

What has to happen is the mind has to go out and buy the home because it's true. *"Eventually, you will buy a home. Eventually, you will refinance. Eventually, you'll list your home."*

So if you're with a client and the client says, *"Well, I don't know if I'm going to buy a home."* You can say, *"Well, eventually you will."*

It's so nonspecific that everyone has to be able to imagine doing it when you put that time period on there.

If somebody says, *"Oh I probably am not going to buy a home."* Here's what you say:

"Oh you probably will."

They go, *"No, I won't."*

But when you say, *"Well, eventually, you probably will,"* they can't say no because eventually could be 100 years.

The mind has to accept it. **It's called "compliance."**

Whenever you are in dialogue, you're looking for lots of small **yeses** in everything that you do. Magic Words or NLP would suggest that when you say "eventually" the mind automatically says, *"Yes. I imagine some time I'll do this. I'm not agreeing that I'm going to do it, but I'm agreeing that sometime I'm doing it."*

This creates some comfortable momentum. Eventually these Magic Words that you're learning right now will trip right off your tongue as easily as your name.

Imagine that.

Inside this dialogue, there's a powerful embedded command. It's "Call me immediately."

We talk a lot about the three things that have to happen in order for someone to introduce you:

1. **They have to notice other people who need your service.**

2. **They have to think of you.**

3. **They have to introduce you.**

So when you're in a dialogue with a person, if you can embed a command you help them notice. You pause, raise your voice, downswing on the command, and pause when you're done saying the embedded command. A downswing is a falling intonation, like you're giving a command.

So it sounds like this:

"Eventually when you do come across a person who you think that I could help, keep in mind that I'm never too busy to help your family your friends and your neighbors in the same way that I was able to help you. So the next time you're in a conversation and the person mentions they want to buy a larger, more spacious home, I'd like you to please (pause and downswing) ***call me immediately*** *(pause). I'm curious what happens when you imagine yourself doing that?"*

The final question isn't asking to do anything.

It's asking to imagine doing something to find out what happens. It's a rhetorical question.

In order for them even to think of the answer, they have to imagine doing it.

"What happens when you imagine calling me?"

Unconsciously, they have to mentally call me in order to give me an answer.

Even if they say, *"Oh I don't know if I'll do that,"* at least they imagined it.

What you and I know is everything happens twice. It happens once mentally, then it has to happen physically.

In many ways, people have to move into the house in their mind before they move into it physically. They have to imagine themselves calling you before they actually call you.

That's just the way the mind works.

It's like a simulator. I have to imagine myself behaving in a way in order for me to actually do the behavior. I have to see myself actually doing it before I'll actually do it.

So when you ask that question: *"Hey, what happens when you imagine yourself selling your home in today's new world?"*

"Oh we would never do that?"

Now, even the fact that they said, *"We'd never do that,"* they had to imagine doing it.

Your job as a consultant is to help people keep moving forward, first mentally, and then physically. It's called future pacing. They have to see themselves in the future before they'll ever step into that future for real.

The more you pace them into the future, the easier it is for them to make those decisions going forward.

"So what happens when you imagine introducing the people you care about to me? That's a great question. *"John, I'm curious. What happens when you imagine introducing the people that you really care about to me?"*

Now, a rhetorical question like this doesn't demand an answer. It's being dealt with at the unconscious level. You're really having an unconscious conversation.

Richard Bandler always says that rapport is having an unconscious conversation with someone, as opposed to a conscious conversation. So when I say, *"What happens when you imagine your furniture in this room?"* they don't even have to answer it. Their mind is already doing it.

"So what happens when you imagine signing the listing contract and achieving all the goals that you set for yourself?"

"So what happens when you imagine yourself putting your home on the market tonight and moving forward with your plans?"

Instead of saying, *"What we need to do now is sign the listing agreement,"* it's easier to say:

"*Mr. and Mrs. Johnson, I'm curious. What happens when you imagine signing the listing agreement right now and getting on with making your dreams of getting a larger, more spacious home for your sons and your daughters so they can have the life that you've always wanted to give them? I'm curious. What happens when you imagine doing that right now?"*

You're NOT saying, *"Sign the listing agreement."*

You're asking them to actually imagine doing it, which means they have to do it in their mind first.

It's very powerful because they have to get compliance first before they actually behave in that direction.

***Exact Ways to Ask 37* – Q Clubs**
To see the video training in the
Magic Words Dojo for this dialogue, go to:
www.byreferralonly.com/WayToAsk37
(you will need to be logged in)

About Joe Stumpf

Joe Stumpf has been in and around the business of real estate coaching and training since 1977.

In 1981, he started his training and coaching company, By Referral Only, which has grown to be one of the largest coaching companies in North America.

Joe Stumpf has a subscription-based company with over 5,000 clients, the purpose of which is to teach the principles, provide the tools and systems, to be highly profitable and at the same time serve others with the heart of a "Super Servant".

Joe Stumpf invests most of his time and energy in creating, writing, and video/audio recording, while his leadership team runs his company's day-to-day operations.

His work has been a wonderful vehicle to express his creativity, as through it he gets to live a life fully expressed as a model of possibility.

It is the perfect forum for him to discover and allow his most authentic self to be publicly shared.

In all of Joe Stumpf's work his intention is to create the next version of himself, one which is more aligned with his soul-purpose.

He has gained a sense of mastery on the goal line, while maintaining a sense of sacred purpose.

Reading, writing, teaching, and coaching is woven into his fabric.

He possesses a beautiful coaching gift of being able to channel insight and awareness to people when they seek clarity and direction in business and life.

He helps people in profound ways so they can experience the shifts they desire as a result of crossing his path.

He views this as his life's purpose.

You're welcome to take a closer look at Joe's work at www.MyByreferralOnly.com.